# BEGINNING WITH OURSELVES

# BEGINNING WITH OURSELVES

In Practice, Theory, and Human Affairs

David E. Hunt

Copyright © 1987 by Brookline Books, Inc.

All rights reserved. No part of this work covered by the copyright may be reproduced or used in any form or by any means—graphic, electronic, or mechanical, including photocopying, recording, taping or information storage and retrieval systems—without the written permission of the publisher.

**Library of Congress Cataloging-in-Publication Data**

Hunt, David E. (David Ellis), 1925–
    Beginning with ourselves in practice, theory, and human affairs.

    Includes bibliographies and index.
    1. Experiential learning. 2. Success.  I. Title.
[DNLM: 1. Self Assessment (Psychology).    BF 697 H939b]
BF318.5.H86  1987      158      86-26431
ISBN 0–914797–33–6
ISBN 0–914797–34–4 (pbk.)

**Canadian Cataloguing in Publication Data**

Hunt, David E., 1925–
    Beginning with ourselves

Bibliography: p.
ISBN 0–7744–0304–7

1. Learning, Psychology of. 2. Self-perception.
3. Psychology, Applied. 4. Life skills.  I. Title

BF318.H86 1987    370.15    C86–094647–9

Published by

**Brookline Books, Inc.**
PO Box 1046              and
Cambridge, MA 02238–1046

**OISE Press**
252 Bloor Street West
Toronto, Ontario M5S 1V6

Cover design by Gord Adams.

**Printed in the United States of America.**

To the memory of my mother,
Lucille Ellis Hunt,

and to my father,
Gayle Jones Hunt,

who both helped me learn
to begin with myself

# Contents

**Preface**   xi

**1. Why Begin with Ourselves?**   1
   Inside-out Psychology
   Stingers
   Plan of the Book

**2. Beginning with Myself:
   Reflections of an Applied Psychologist**   9
   There is Nothing Like an Experiment (1948–1949)
   There is Nothing Like a Theory (1949–1961)
   There is Nothing so Practical as a Good Theory (1961–1971)
   Application of a Matching Model (1971–1976)
   There is Nothing so Theoretical as Good Practice (1976–present)
   Overcoming Resistance from Inside and Outside

**3. Beginning with Ourselves in Learning Style**   37
   How Are We Alike and How Are We Different?
   What Is Learning Style?
   Matching in the Moment
   Identifying Your Own Learning Style
   The Strange Case of the Missing ATIs
   The Marketing of Learning Style
   Demystifying Learning Style

**4. Teachers and Counselors Begin with Themselves**   53
   Beginning with Practitioners
   Why Should Practitioners Bring Out Their Theories?
   The Return of the Rep Test
   George Kelly, Meet Kurt Lewin!
   How To Be Your Own Best Theorist II
   A Counselor Brings Out Her Theories
   Bringing Out Your Matching Models
   Bringing Out Your Metaphors
   Personal Theories of Teaching
   Practitioners' Experiencing and Overcoming Resistance

## Contents

**5. Consultants and Supervisors Begin with Themselves**    85

     The Problem of Three Populations
     Actions Speak Louder Than Words: The Exemplification Principle
     A Consultant Brings Out Her Theories
     Becoming My Own Best Theorist
     Consultants Bring Out Their Models and Metaphors
     Identifying Patterns of Consultation
     Consultants' Experiencing and Overcoming Resistance

**6. Theorists and Researchers Begin with Themselves**    105

     Theorists Are Persons, Too
     Practice Makes Perfect? No, Practice Makes Theory
     First Person Singular
     What About Common Sense?
     The New Three Rs and the UFO Model
     How To Be Your Own Best Researcher
     Overcoming Resistance and Redefining Psychology

**7. Beginning with Ourselves in Practice-Theory Relations**    123

     Image of Practice-Theory Relations
     Implementation as Mutual Adaptation: The RAND Study
     Studies in Mutual Adaptation
     The New Three Rs as Guides for Theorists Working with Practitioners
     Beginning with Ourselves in Staff Development
     Overcoming Resistance in Changing the Image of Practice-Theory Relations

**8. Beginning with Ourselves in Interpersonal Relations**    145

     A Mutual Adaptation View of Interpersonal Relations
     Variations on a Theme by Kolb
     Applying the Cycle: C-RE-A-T-E
     In the Beginning There Was Direct Experience

**Appendix: How To Be Your Own Best Theorist**    163

**References**    173

**Index**    179

# Acknowledgements

Grateful acknowledgement is extended to the following for granting permission to reprint excerpts:

Harper and Row Publishers for permission to reprint the poem "Melinda Mae" from *Where the Sidewalk Ends* by Shel Silverstein (1974).

Elliott Eisner for permission to quote from his paper "Can Educational Research Inform Educational Practice?" (*Phi Delta Kappan*, 1984, 65, 447–452).

David Kolb for permitting the reprinting of figures and text from "Toward an Applied Theory of Experiential Learning" in C. Cooper (Ed.) *Studies of Group Process*, (New York: Wiley, 1975, pp. 33–57) and the Learning Style Inventory (Boston: McBer, 1976).

Dell Publishers for permission to quote from Kirschenbaum, H.K. *On Becoming Carl Rogers* (New York: Delacorte, 1979).

Dennis Fox for permission to reprint the table from "Personal Theories of Teaching" (*Studies in Higher Education, 8*, 151–163).

# Preface

This book describes how practitioners, theorists, and nonprofessionals can begin with themselves. Practitioners include teachers, counselors, therapists, social workers, nurses, consultants, supervisors, and trainers who are encouraged to bring out their experienced knowledge about their practice. Theorists and researchers in psychology, education, and other social sciences are encouraged to bring out their personal and practical knowledge rather than their theoretical knowledge. When practitioners and theorists bring out their experienced knowledge, they have a common basis for improving communication and working relations. Nonprofessionals should also find these approaches appropriate with only slight revisions. In addition, all readers are encouraged to apply these approaches to their everyday lives as parents and marital partners.

New ideas are conventionally presented on theoretical and research grounds. By contrast, I make my case for beginning with ourselves almost exclusively on practical grounds: Do these ideas help you in your everyday life? Do they fit in with your own experience? Applying these practical criteria requires that you hold theoretical and research criteria in abeyance (to be applied later if you wish) while you consider their practical value. Recently I heard an actor on a movie preview say, "This ain't no book, this is the real thing" and I smiled as I realized that this was close to the mark. This *is* a book, but I hope it is also the real thing. As you read these ideas, try them out to see how they work and then decide for yourself.

The development of my ideas has benefitted through working and learning with graduate students/colleagues in our psychology of teaching program. To the several hundred experienced practitioners who, as graduate students in my learning styles class, brought out their implicit theories, I am very grateful, especially so to four of them—Jane Gow, Maureen Lanois, Barbara Rosen-Schreiber, and Mary Shawcross—who agreed to "go public" and allow their implicit theories to appear here as examples, both in spirit and substance, of practitioners' beginning with themselves. To those experienced practitioners who have temporarily become researchers as they pursue their doctoral theses in psychology of teaching, I am indebted for a different reason. If they are to base their doctoral theses on their own experienced knowledge, they need a rationale for doing so, and I hope this book provides the academic legitimacy for their building on this practice. I especially want to thank one of these former doctoral students, Mary Hookey, for allowing me to use portions of her doctoral thesis.

More than a dozen granting agencies have supported my work during the thirty years spanned in this book, and special thanks are due to the Research and Development office of the Ontario Institute for Studies in Education and to the Social Science and Humanities

Research Council, especially for supporting Studies in Mutual Adaptation (0929) from 1979 to 1984.

I am deeply grateful to my secretary, Maria Tocheri, for typing the several drafts of this manuscript with expertise and good cheer. Donna Thompson was a most helpful copyeditor. Thanks to Peter Chisholm for his work on the cover design. Finally, I appreciate my wife, Jan, for her support and good humor, which helped make writing this book a joy.

# 1
# Why Begin with Ourselves?

My theme, beginning with ourselves, is based on George Kelly's belief that every person is a psychologist. Psychology is the study of human affairs, and each of us has a wealth of knowledge based on a lifetime of direct experience in this area. Psychologists and other social scientists investigate this subject through formal theories and research, but much more knowledge is potentially available from those of you who are not psychologists. Your common sense ideas and your unexpressed theories, growing out of your own personal experience, provide enormously rich sources of knowledge about human affairs. By beginning with yourself, therefore, you are taking advantage of this rich reservoir—tapping what you know about yourself and others to bring out your experienced knowledge on topics that psychologists would call interpersonal relations, self-awareness, individual differences, teaching and learning, and so on.

My ideas on beginning with ourselves originated when I was working with classroom teachers to help them adapt to the wide variation in learning styles among their students. Working as a practical theorist, I became dissatisfied with the conventional view that if a logical theory were developed and verified through research, then it could be directly applied to classroom practice. The abstract idea that "theory leads to practice" is logical enough, but it did not offer a satisfactory account of how we were actually working together. Describing our work together in this abstract way cut us off from our direct experience, thereby removing us from the realities of the practice we were trying to improve. My initial attempts to correct this situation were summarized by the titles of three papers I wrote at that time. Experienced practitioners were encouraged to bring out what they knew from their practical experience in "Teachers Are Psychologists, Too" (Hunt, 1976a). Practical theorists were similarly directed to identify their personal beliefs and ideas about what goes on in practice in "Theorists Are Persons, Too" (Hunt, 1978a). Although I did not understand it clearly at that time, it seems that when both practitioner and theorist identify their experienced knowledge, a sound, practical basis for communicating and working together is formed. Bringing out my own personal beliefs (not my formal theories) set the foundation for communicating more effectively with classroom teachers who had also identified their unexpressed implicit theories, as shown in "Theory-to-Practice as Persons-in-Relation" (Hunt, 1977b).

## Inside-Out Psychology

Simple as it seems, beginning with yourself is not so easy to put into practice. To begin with yourself requires that you temporarily suspend your belief in psychologist-as-expert and your belief that social science will solve human problems. It is an *Inside-out* psychology, rooted in your own experience, and it is totally opposite to the traditional *Outside-in* approach which leaves human affairs to the experts. My suggestion to start Inside-out does not require that you completely reject Outside-in, or formal, psychology. It calls for Inside-out to come first, because, among other things, this approach provides a valuable base from which to consider Outside-in information.

I did not realize when I began to use Inside-out psychology how much resistance I would encounter. I consider this resistance—which takes the forms of outside obstacles as well as internal blocks—in detail later. For now I want to comment briefly on the resistance—if only to emphasize that I do not want you to stop reading at this point because your resistance has taken over.

If you are one of my psychologist colleagues, then you are likely to experience at least some resistance, because Inside-out requires that you either temporarily forget or permanently abandon the psychologist-as-expert role. Letting go of this established role, however, opens an exciting alternative for you. For example, writing about psychology as I am doing is writing about myself and my personal beliefs, an obvious point but one that is not usually acknowledged by mainstream psychology; yet, I find that as one person writing to other participants in the human venture, the effect is liberating, exhilarating, and

## Why Begin with Ourselves

revitalizing. I don't have to maintain an artificial, impersonal role, and I am more likely to trust myself. I hope that those of you who are applied psychologists and practical theorists will come to agree with me.

If you are an experienced practitioner—classroom teacher, counselor, or consultant—then you probably have to deal with another form of resistance. Like most practitioners, you have likely been professionally socialized to rely on expert authority rather than your own experience. (For those of you who have not, that's great!) Therefore, you will need to regain your trust in yourself and your experience to adopt the Inside-out approach and begin with yourself. I do not maintain that because you are a practitioner your implicit theory is completely valid or that your experienced knowledge is necessarily better than all formal theories, only that identifying your implicit theory of practice will create a foundation for determining its validity and value compared with formal theories.

Those of you who are neither theorists nor practitioners also must deal with resistance. Like the experienced practitioner, you have probably been conditioned to rely on experts for knowledge about human affairs. Headlines show that we are expected to depend on expert judgment, research evidence, and survey results to guide us in our everyday lives: "Experts agree that the poor are more prone to illness, more unhappy;" "Experiments show that older people have poorer memories," and "Survey indicates that marital happiness is associated with couples being good friends." Now these would be funny if they were not true. As a lay person, what you must do is cut through the mystique of the experts, the experiments, and the surveys as royal roads to knowledge about how to live your life; you have to re-establish trust in yourself and your experience.

I was not kidding earlier when I said that I did not want you to stop reading simply out of resistance to my initial ideas, so allow me to request your good will. I invite you initially to accept my idea of beginning with ourselves as an article of faith; then, as I try to make my case for it, throughout the book I invite you to "try it on for size," as George Kelly would say. In addition to considering the logic of and evidence for my ideas and approaches, I invite you to try them out in your lives to see how they work. I do not ask that you suspend your critical judgment, only that you give these proposals a try for their practical value in your work and in your life. As you try to begin with yourself, be aware of whether you experience increased self-understanding, improved communication, or a clearer basis on which to evaluate suggestions from others. See how it goes. Even if you fail to notice any benefits, you will not have lost anything.

Before summarizing the chapters in the book, I will first make a few comments about my style of writing and thinking.

# Stingers

I like to use short, stinging statements like "Every person is a psychologist" to organize and communicate my ideas. These statements might be called mottos, maxims, epigrams, aphorisms, axioms, or just one-liners, but in this book I call them *stingers*. I invented this colloquial term because stingers have a very special meaning to me. They usually describe basic assumptions, and they may be expressed as statements ("There is nothing so practical as a good theory"), phrases ("The problem of three populations"), initials ("The New Three R's"; "The UFO model"), or even in the form of Haiku. Stingers come from others or from myself, and I may transform another person's stinger for my purposes, e.g., "Every psychologist is a person."

## Stingers Help Me Understand My Ideas and Work

Kurt Lewin's motto "There is nothing so practical as a good theory" became the stinger that guided and focused a portion of my work, as I describe in Chapter 2. Like Seymour Sarason's idea of an axiom, a stinger can be unconscious and unexpressed. However, in this case I was very aware of the Lewinian stinger, carrying the banner high and using it explicitly to evaluate my work. George Kelly's basic assumption that "Every person is a psychologist" is the stinger that underlies the ideas I present in this book.

## Stingers Help Communicate with Practitioners

Experienced practitioners suffer because they lack their own language to describe and communicate about their craft. Stingers speak in practitioners' language; because they are free of jargon, they can be understood quickly and intuitively. This does not mean that every stinger is true or that every practitioner will agree with every stinger, only that a stinger will be quickly grasped. Because I write primarily to practitioners and secondarily to theorists and researchers, I am for clarity through intuitive understanding rather than through technical precision. Indeed, my choice of the term "stinger" itself indicates my aim for clarity through plain, colloquial language. At their best, as in George Kelly's stinger "hardening of the categories," stingers transcend their verbal form and become powerful, nonverbal images.

## Stingers Show
## How Others Have Influenced My Ideas

My three heroes in psychology are Kurt Lewin, George Kelly, and Seymour Sarason, and their influence on my ideas is clearly illustrated by my use of stingers. In addition to those stingers I already mentioned, I like Kurt Lewin's "If you want to understand something, try to change it" (Lewin, 1951); George Kelly's suggestion "If you want to know what is wrong with the client, always ask him—he might tell you" (Kelly, 1955); and Seymour Sarason's "myth of unlimited resources" (Sarason, 1972), which, like every good stinger, is worth a thousand words.

## Stingers Can Be Transformed

I find that transforming a stinger often produces a strong antidote for my own "hardening of the categories." Reversing a stinger, as in "There is nothing so theoretical as good practice," produced a transformed stinger that quite literally turned my work around, as described in Chapter 2. Transforming a stinger also helps us understand the original stinger more clearly.

A transformed stinger, such as "Theorists are persons, too," *really* stings. In the case of a chapter I wrote using this phrase as the title (Hunt, 1978a), the idea was dismissed as a simple play on words, which I took to be a strong resistance to my stinging suggestions. Transformed stingers may sound funny at first, but I state them with a serious purpose. As someone once said, you do not have to be solemn to be serious. *That's* a nice stinger for you, and it leads to my final point.

## Stingers Are Fun

I enjoy thinking and writing in stingers, and I do not pretend to understand why. Perhaps they give me some comic relief from the otherwise ponderous and impossible task of psychology in its attempt to understand human affairs. They may appeal to my comic sub-personality, which wants to spout one-liners. I really have no idea—they are just fun!

During the writing and rewriting of this section on stingers, I was continually aware of my "Little Professor" and the need to keep him in check. He wanted to do such things as place the stinger in its historical perspective, rationalize stinger transformation as meeting the appropriate criteria for transformative processes, present a comparative analysis of stingers versus metaphors, and insert numerous bibliographical citations and explanatory footnotes. Some of you may wish that I had given in to my Little Professor; the problem is that if I had done so, I would never have used the word "stinger" in the first place. I would have been much too worried about its colloquial imprecision and its academic legitimacy. As it stands, the medium is indeed the message.

As it happened, the term "stinger" flashed into my mind when I first wrote that I like "short, stinging statements." I had never used nor even heard the word before (except to describe the final, emphatic note in a Sousa march). Using it here seems right for me, and I hope it works for you. (For those of you who are really concerned about bibliographic citations, rest assured that I have not abandoned my Little Professor forever. He will serve them up in due course.)

## Plan of the Book

Actions speak louder than words so in Chapter 2 I begin with myself to illustrate how you can do the same. In Chapter 3, a discussion of learning style illustrates Inside-out versus Outside-in approaches and how they can be combined.

Chapters 4, 5, and 6 address specific audiences. Chapter 4 is written especially for practitioners (teachers, counselors, social workers, nurses, etc.); Chapter 5 for those who work with practitioners (consultants, supervisors, and trainers); and Chapter 6 is directed to theorists and researchers (and to those practitioners who temporarily become researchers in conducting their doctoral research). These three chapters describe specific Inside-out approaches—"How To Be Your Own Best Theorist" (Hunt, 1980a) and "How To Be Your Own Best Researcher"—and include examples of the exercises used by each professional group to bring out their implicit theories. You may wish to go directly to the one written for your group, but I hope you will read all three. I believe that doing so will help you understand the views of other colleagues, which, in turn, will improve communication and working relations.

Chapter 7 describes how to begin with ourselves in practice-theory relations, with special emphasis on beginning with practice to facilitate communication and working relations between practitioners and theorists. In Chapter 8 I discuss beginning with ourselves in interpersonal relationships. There I adapt a model of experiential learning to promote understanding in interpersonal transactions and to provide a means for people to share what they know about human affairs to help each other with their concerns.

Throughout these chapters I develop my case to redefine psychology and the role of psychologists. In contrast to the current role of psychologist-as-expert, I propose that psychologists create open, reciprocal climates in order to enhance their own and others' self-knowledge, which will facilitate communication and permit them to try out their knowledge in action.

# 2
# Beginning with Myself: Reflections of an Applied Psychologist

In this chapter, I follow my own advice and begin with myself. I borrow Ira Progoff's concept of "stepping stones" (Progoff, 1975), which offers the advantage of summarizing the highlights of my 35 years as an applied psychologist. These stepping stones will show how my ideas have developed without including unnecessary autobiographical detail. Besides illustrating the developmental base of my ideas, I would also like to show the benefits we derive from beginning with ourselves—specifically, how this approach enhances our self-understanding, improves our ability to communicate, and provides the foundation for changing our actions.

When I first thought about "going public" with this autobiographical chapter, I felt uneasy. Then I realized that most of us feel this way at the prospect of disclosing our own ideas and beliefs. I discovered that my resistance was long-standing, having been trained and professionally socialized against revealing my personal views (at least while wearing my psychologist's hat). As I struggled to overcome these internal obstacles, I became aware of several specific reasons for my resistance: defensiveness, unwillingness to trust myself, limited awareness of my feelings, and lack of know-how about personal and professional reflection. At the end of this chapter, you should be able to estimate my batting average at knocking away these obstacles. Dealing with this resistance is a continuous struggle, yet I think I have made some progress or I would not have been able to write this book.

I have been writing about practicing Inside-out psychology for the past ten years and have been fascinated by the enormous *external* resistance from mainstream psychology and the educational research establishment. Their double-barreled message came though loud and clear: "Stop this tender-minded nonsense and get back to being psychologist-as-expert where you belong." They were telling me to return to my proper place as an Outside-in psychologist who retains the power and control associated with professional expertise. Aware of the strong resistance to beginning with myself, both internally and externally, I conclude this chapter with a summary of the sources of resistance and how I have tried to overcome them.

My "Little Optimist" wants to restate the last two paragraphs more positively—to begin with ourselves requires both internal resources and external support. A number of suggestions are offered throughout this and later chapters to identify and use your internal resources. Finding and/or developing a setting that provides the necessary external support for beginning with ourselves is more challenging, but I offer some suggestions on dealing with this issue.

As I organized my stepping stones, I found it most puzzling that although my master's thesis (Hunt, 1951) was the first research study conducted on George Kelly's theory that "Every person is a psychologist" (Kelly, 1955), my work for the next 25 years made no reference to Kelly's powerful stinger or his theory of personal constructs. Not until 1976, when I published "Teachers Are Psychologists, Too" (Hunt, 1976a), did I return to this central idea, an idea that became the basic theme for this book. What took me so long? Since this discontinuity in my stepping stones aptly illustrates how both internal and external conditions are needed to bring out an idea, let me briefly summarize why I think this 25-year lapse occurred.

First, on the *internal* side: In 1951 I did not know enough about the meaning and implication of "Every person is a psychologist" to carry it through to beginning with ourselves. (I did not even trust the results of my somewhat unorthodox master's thesis enough to submit it for publication.) Second, on the *external* side: In the early 1950s there was great faith in psychology-as-science (Outside-in), which would have strongly resisted the Inside-out approach. For example, George Kelly's two-volume work, *The Psychology of Personal Constructs,* published in 1955, received very little acceptance until the 1970s—and then primarily in England. Even if I had possessed the necessary personal moxie to try, my thesis would probably not have been published, and I would certainly have had difficulty in finding a job as an Inside-out psychologist. The stinger "An idea whose time has come" is only half right; it emphasizes the external conditions. The idea itself must be internally developed so it is ready when its time comes.

I describe my work in five phases: (1) There is nothing like an experiment (1948–1949); (2) There is nothing like a theory (1949–1961); (3) There is nothing so practical as a good theory (1961–1971); (4) Application of a matching model (1971–1976); and (5) There is nothing so theoretical as good practice (1976–present). The stepping stones within these phases show both the steps I took in developing my ideas and the steps I did not take.

# There Is Nothing Like an Experiment (1948–1949)

Beginning with my introductory psychology course, which emphasized psychology-as-science, and continuing with other undergraduate courses, I was increasingly led to believe that knowledge about human affairs must come either from formal psychological theory or from rigorous experimental research. It was not until later that I actually tried my hand at psychological theory but, like most psychology majors, I was indoctrinated in psychology-as-experiment in the senior course in experimental psychology. It was in this course that I can first remember trying to think and write in "psychologese." I was very keen on doing well since I had applied to go to graduate school, and my grade in experimental psychology would be an important factor.

The major assignment in this course was to design and conduct an experiment on a new topic. My experience on this assignment shows that even when an Inside-out approach is more appropriate, psychology relies on experimental evidence from Outside-in. Because I was a long-standing jazz fan, I chose "the emotional value of music" as my topic. I proposed to investigate through a controlled experiment how jazz musicians, with their improvised solos, are able to communicate specific states of emotion to the listener. I was personally convinced of the truth of my hypothesis through my own listening experience. I vowed to bring to bear all the rigor and precision of the experimental method to prove my point. I remember my excitement at having the opportunity to apply the tools of my soon-to-be profession to my favorite avocation.

I will spare you most of the details of this pretentious exercise except to say that I followed the axioms of the scientific method. I prepared my research materials on a phonograph record (this was before the portable tape recorder); variables were controlled (only jazz trumpet passages were recorded); responses of the subjects (Ss) were controlled objectively (they were asked to match each of the eight passages with eight emotional descriptions); and the passages were counterbalanced (they were alternately played in reverse order). After running thirty Ss through my procedure, I analyzed the responses and summarized the rather ambiguous findings in an almost incomprehensible, highly qualified jargon—which concluded with a call for more research.

Leafing through the yellowed pages of this old research report, I noticed a daring departure from the conventional Outside-in form. Because the master record onto which I had recorded the eight trumpet passages had some remaining space, I had filled in the remainder of the 12-inch master with Charlie Parker's solo on "Lover Man," a rendition that I had always felt to be the epitome of emotional expressiveness. Since this unscientific additional solo was there, I concluded my experimental sessions by playing the Parker solo and asking the subjects what feeling they thought he was expressing. Of the thirty subjects, two-thirds described Parker's passage as depressed or anxious, which, as I reported, "provided some tentative support for the hypothesis." What I did not include in my report were three subjects whose responses I can still remember because they zeroed in on his feelings. They made such statements as "He sounds like he's going crazy" and "They'd better lock him up." Several years later I learned that immediately after Parker played this solo, he suffered a complete mental breakdown and was hospitalized for several months (Russell, 1972, p. 221). I did not have this "hard data" about his emotional state in 1948. Besides, only 3 subjects out of 30 mentioned that he was going crazy, so I omitted this from my report. I was learning my trade.

# There Is Nothing Like a Theory (1949 – 1961)

When I began graduate training in clinical psychology at Ohio State University in 1949, there were very high hopes that psychology-as-science would improve the lives of everyone. We were all in the midst of the giddy optimism following World War II. Especially for those of us who were returning veterans going to school on the G.I. Bill (I had been a machine gunner in Patton's Third Army), the challenge to improve the human condition seemed almost a personal responsibility. The New Clinical Psychology, born just after World War II, offered hope for meeting this challenge. It was based on logical theory and rigorous research, and required personality theories from which to derive experiments which, in turn, would inform clinical practice. How fortunate that we graduate students were in the clinical program at Ohio State in the early 1950s, when two major personality theories were being developed: George Kelly's personal construct theory (Kelly, 1955) and Julian Rotter's social learning theory (Rotter, 1954). Heady stuff indeed; we had the chance not only to observe the evolution of a major personality theory but also to be a part of its development.

I clearly remember George Kelly, then director of the clinical program, welcoming us with the indelible stinger "The only thing we know about the clinical psychology of the future is that it will be different." In many ways the program was based on this belief. The only element that was not subject to change was the belief in clinical psychology-as-science, which was firmly rooted in personality theory. For example, although I remember Kelly's stinger as "Every person is a psychologist," his preferred way of expressing it was "man-as-scientist." I was attracted to Kelly's ideas and joined his research team in 1950 to pursue the promise of his then sketchy theory for applying scientific approaches and concepts to investigate the individual's personal understanding or personal constructs.

## Master's Thesis: The Rep Test (1951)

Since every respectable personality theory must have its own personality measures, we developed the first version of the Role Concept Repertory Test, or Rep Test, which I revised much later for "How To Be Your Own Best Theorist" (Hunt, 1980a). Based on the first Rep Test, my master's thesis was not only the first Rep Test study but also the first in the theory of personal constructs.

My thesis was a curious combination of Inside-out and Outside-in (or what Kelly called "ideographic" and "nomothetic") in that I tried to investigate the test-retest reliability of the Rep Test, or what I called "conceptual consistency." Then as now, one of the first criteria for a psychological test was its "stability" (i.e., Does it yield the same results at two points in time?). I therefore administered the Rep Test to subjects on two occasions one week apart using alternate forms (different role titles) and considered the degree to which the content of the second list of constructs remained the same.

I immediately encountered the problem of defining what the "same" concept was (e.g., Is it the same when "honest" is used one week and "trustworthy" the next?). Rather than simply calling this issue "defining sameness," my Boy Scientist emerged and coined it "functional equivalence." (If you can't solve a problem, at least give it an abstract title.) After struggling with the analysis of sameness, I eventually reported that the percentage of agreement was 68. I remember longing to express the test-retest relationship in terms of some very complicated statistical index defined by a Greek letter but, try as I might, I was stuck with a simple percentage. (I think it was partly due to my dissatisfaction with the unscientific nature of the percent index that I did not submit my thesis for publication in a journal.)

Kelly's theory was clearly rich in implications for clinical practice (e.g., his suggestion that clients "try on for size" a new construct through fixed role therapy) as well as for research. It permitted testing a general idea by evaluating its application to specific persons. For example, the hypothesis that when one is trying to abandon an old role, personal threat will be experienced from another person who either exemplifies that old role or expects us to act according to the old, rejected role was tested by considering each participant's own specific personal constructs (Landfield, 1954). With all its richness, personal construct theory went almost unnoticed by mainstream psychology in North America until British psychologists Bannister and Fransella "revived" Kelly's theory in 1971 with their publication *Inquiring Man* (Bannister & Fransella, 1971). For reasons that historians of psychology may someday understand, Kelly's work remains much more popular in Britain and parts of Europe than in North America.

## Internship (1952)

Having completed my master's thesis and the remainder of my doctoral course work, I spent one year as a psychological intern at the Bureau of Juvenile Research, where my outlook necessarily shifted from theory to practice. In contrast to many field placements, my case load was reasonable (12 to 15 youngsters), and there was considerable time to form impressions of each one since the average stay was about two months. The setting was excellent for learning about assessment because there was ample time not only to test each case but also to observe and to initiate short-term therapy. However, in writing the summary reports and making recommendations for my first cases, I realized that my entire assessment had to be compressed into a single recommendation with essentially two options: foster home placement or institutional treatment.

I experienced *déjà vu* in writing one of my first reports during internship. The experience was very similar to one I had when working as a psychometrist at the state mental hospital in my hometown the summer before I started graduate school. In that hospital setting I gave a large test battery (Rorschach, TAT, Wechsler-Bellevue, Draw-a-Person, etc.), all of which had to be correlated to form a psychodynamic portrait that no one ever read. There were only two options for action in the hospital: to administer electric shock therapy or not. In both settings, the assessment function seemed to be almost unrelated or, at best, poorly correlated with recommendations for action. This discrepancy between diagnosis and treatment has preoccupied me ever since. (Later I suggested the term "accessibility characteristic" as a concept to bridge the gap.)

During my internship, I discussed this problem with my colleague and lifelong friend Ralph Dunlap. We decided that we should start with the options available—foster home and institutional placement—to consider what characteristics might be associated with a youngster's success in one setting or the other. Then we would try to assess our youngsters in terms of those characteristics. We tried working with the tentative assumption that those who prosper in foster homes are more likely to be adult-oriented in terms of social approval while those who function better in an institutional setting are more peer-oriented. We therefore assessed, observed, and worked with our assigned cases on this basis to determine whether they seemed to be primarily peer- or adult-oriented. We did not have the opportunity to find out whether our assumption was valid or not but at least we were able to conduct our assessment activities in a manner relevant to our recommendations for placement.

## Doctoral Dissertation: Social Learning Theory (1953)

I joined Julian Rotter's research team for my doctoral research for a variety of reasons. Perhaps the most important was that many of my close friends (Harry Schroder, Ralph Dunlap, B.J. Fitzgerald, Sandy Dean, and Al Casteneda) were on Rotter's team. I might have continued with Kelly for my dissertation, but I suppose that I wanted the best of both worlds.

Rotter's social learning theory was a personality theory of generalized formulas, and my dissertation attempted to validate one of them, that "changes in goal object preference will be directly related to the expectancy of subsequent reinforcement" (Hunt, 1953). My methodology can be colloquially summarized as follows: After finding out how well fourth-grade boys like a group of certain toys, I praised them when they played with specific ones to see if it affected how well they liked them afterward. The results were generally positive, so the dissertation was published (Hunt, 1955). What I did *not* report here or in my journal publication was a fact that I was only dimly aware of at the time, and that was probably more important than what I reported. Most of the reinforcement effects came from lower-class boys, primarily from an inner-city school, while middle-class boys from another school were less responsive to my verbal praise. In the mid-1950s, it was not fashionable to consider variation among Ss; it was regarded as "error variance." Twenty years later, Sullivan and I tried to redress this imbalance in *Between Psychology and Education* (Hunt & Sullivan, 1974), arguing to include the person when making psychological interpretations.

Viewed 30 years later, Rotter's social learning theory has not fared as well as Kelly's theory, which has become increasingly well known. Most psychologists think that social learning was concocted by Bandura and Walters (1963) and remember Rotter primarily for his I-E scale (Internal vs. External Control of Responsibility, 1966). At the time, however, my rigorous doctoral dissertation served me well in obtaining my first job in the department of psychology at Yale, the center of scientific analysis of reinforcement theory.

## Yale (1953–1959)

A few highlights of my six years at Yale stand out. First, I was next door to Seymour Sarason, director of the clinical training program, who, although I'm sure he was not aware of it, provided me with an awesome role model of what a Yale faculty member is supposed to be. Shortly after I arrived, he completed one of his many books, *The Clinical Interaction* (Sarason, 1954), which he wrote in less than two months with very few changes from the first draft. I was so in awe of his many talents that, even though he could not have been more friendly, it was not until the early 1970s that I could begin to think of myself as measuring up to him as a colleague. Then we became good friends. He is not only one of my heroes but also, more importantly, a true friend. For that I am extremely fortunate.

My job at Yale involved teaching graduate students to administer such psychological tests as the Wechsler, Binet, and the Thematic Apperception Test. I found myself faced with the same old puzzler: What purpose lies behind these test reports? From my experience during my internship I felt the students should know. Another junior colleague, Joel Davitz, and I became sufficiently concerned that we made a bold move; we actually asked some of the professionals (psychiatrists, social workers, etc.) their reasons for requesting these tests (i.e., what specific decisions they might make on the basis of the test reports). I wish that we had taken this project more seriously and recorded some of our findings. As it was, we were both too preoccupied with getting our careers started to realize that what we thought were "no results" were actually quite important. Most of the responses were: "Just give us the usual psychodynamic interpretation as you have been doing and don't worry about it." In retrospect, I think that our questioning probably embarrassed many of the professionals because they had not really thought about their reasons for testing.

Fifteen years later, Lee Shulman coined one of my favorite stingers to express this puzzle: "We will never understand person-environment combinations as long as we continue to measure persons with micrometers and environments with divining rods." (Shulman, 1970, p. 374). I wish I had said that! Even if I had, however, I doubt that it would have made much difference in the mid-1950s because it would have raised uncomfortable questions about the fundamental, unspoken assumption on which the scientific basis of the New Clinical Psychology was being built—that detailed psychodiagnostic reports were valuable because they were scientific and objective.

Another recollection from my Yale days is my collaboration with my lifelong friend and colleague Harry Schroder, who had come to Princeton from Ohio State, where we had first met. Being junior faculty members in the Ivy League in those days of "up or out" and "publish or perish" was not easy and our collaboration provided both personal support and professional cooperation. We conducted experiments simultaneously in New Haven and Princeton, then compared our findings, and submitted for publication only those experiments in which we found the same results.

The most popular topic for social psychologists at that time was social conformity; they were conducting experiments to show how people-in-general could be influenced to change their views and conform. By contrast, our experiments (Hunt & Schroder, 1958; Schroder & Hunt, 1957, 1958) showed how different persons respond to different kinds of social influence, such as informational influence or majority opinion. Our suggestion that psychologists consider what these differential effects are in their experiments went unheeded because psychology-as-science was then seeking general laws applicable to everyone. (Remember, this was long before the stinger "Different strokes for different folks" was invented.) However, our collaborative work on differential effects set the stage for *Conceptual Systems and Personality Organization* (Harvey, Hunt, & Schroder, 1961).

## Conceptual Systems and Personality Organization (1961)

Conceptual Systems Theory provided an interactive account of how persons might become more independent. This had become a very important concern in the United States at that time—the post-Sputnik era—when originality meant getting ahead of the Russians. From the viewpoint of contemporary concerns, the book was well timed. As we put it in our concluding comments:

> The problems discussed in this chapter are important not only for the individual, in terms of his self-adequacy and experience of psychological well-being, but also for a culture like ours, which in the present process of increasing its valuation of creativity and inventiveness, seeks ways in which such activities can be encouraged. (p. 346)

# There Is Nothing So Practical as a Good Theory (1961–1971)

The 1961 publication of *Conceptual Systems and Personality Organization* marked a professional turning point for me. For the next 15 years I worked to show that there was nothing so practical as Conceptual Systems Theory. It was certainly the right time for a sometime psychological theorist like myself to become an applied psychologist. Piaget's ideas were being considered as guides to practice (J.M. Hunt, 1961) and many academic psychologists (such as Bruner and Kohlberg) were turning their attention to the world of practice.

The New Frontier and the War on Poverty in the United States produced many social action programs at this time, like Head Start, Upward Bound, the Peace Corps, and the Teacher Corps. These large-scale programs were launched in a hurry, resulting in an almost desperate need for an applied theory that would serve as a blueprint for program development and evaluation. The call "Theorists, please apply" went out and I responded with enthusiasm.

## Matching Through Homogeneous Grouping (1962–1964)

I moved to Syracuse University in 1959, partly to work in the newly created Youth Development Center (YDC), an interdisciplinary research center dedicated to bringing the knowledge acquired from the social sciences to bear on the problems of inner-city youth. In tune with the times (the War on Poverty had just begun) and supported by the Ford Foundation and the Office of Economic Opportunity (OEO), the YDC was an ideal opportunity for me to apply Conceptual Systems Theory—more specifically, the Conceptual Level (CL) matching model that I had developed to improve the educational experience of inner-city, disadvantaged youngsters.

The idea of matching one's teaching approach to the needs of students is certainly not new, although experienced practitioners are too busy to bother to express their matching ideas formally. In the case of the CL matching model, I made the matching process explicit through an "If ... then ..." statement, linking the student's orientation with the appropriate approach. Later, in 1971, I extended matching principles to other accessibility characteristics, but in the early 1960s the explicit formulation of meeting student needs by following a matching model was a novel approach.

The CL matching principle links the person's conceptual level, or level of complexity, with the appropriate degree of structure required: *if* the person has low CL, *then* use high structure; *if* the person has high CL, *then* low structure or a variety of structures are appropriate. This simple principle is based on the notion that the degree of structure in the learning environment should complement the student's need for it. Initially, I made my case for the validity of this matching principle through simple logic and common-sense appeal; later, several dozen experiments supported it as well (Miller, 1981). In addition to this version of the matching principle, which was applied under contemporaneous or immediate circumstances, it was also expressed in developmental terms (e.g., *if*

# Beginning with Myself

a person is at Stage X, *then* provide this environment to encourage development to the next stage). In the developmental account, persons were thought to proceed through three stages to the highest conceptual level of self-direction and autonomy.

As luck would have it, in 1962 Mario Fantini and Gerry Weinstein initiated a large-scale educational program aimed at the inner-city youth of Syracuse and my CL matching model was a natural blueprint for improving the classroom experience of these disadvantaged youngsters. My first venture as an applied theorist, therefore, was to form homogeneous classroom groups of ninth-grade students on the basis of their CL (Hunt, 1966a) or their need for structure.

Homogeneous grouping of students according to CL (or any other characteristic) is attractive to educational administrators because it seems to offer increased efficiency of teacher resources. Teachers working with students who have similar needs are presumably able to meet those needs more efficiently and effectively. At least, so goes the argument that I used at the time. Later I was to learn that homogeneous grouping by need for structure (or any other characteristic) can also inadvertently lead to teachers' downplaying the importance of helping students develop—that is, teachers continuously "spoon-feed" students needing structure so that they never learn self-responsibility.

Upon becoming aware of this possibility and other potential disadvantages of homogeneous classroom grouping, I realized the possible negative and unintended effects of the application of any theory. Put simply, a developmental theory such as Conceptual Systems can be used for quite distinct purposes, either to encourage development, helping persons realize their potential, or to control or restrict the person on the basis of present style. In other words, it can be used to facilitate or restrain development. Had I realized this fact in 1962, I might well have abandoned the effort, although I'm not sure that this would have been the best move. In any case, every applied theorist should be aware that his blueprints may be used for a number of purposes, some of them unintended.

Another feature of this experience is worth noting, though I was unaware, it was the first time I took teachers' implicit theories into account. When the teachers first began to work with the three CL homogeneous classes they were not informed of the CL scores of their groups. They simply worked with them according to how they experienced each group, and observers noted any differences in teacher response to each class. It was a pilot study in "student pull" (Hunt, 1976b). The observers recorded that in most cases these experienced teachers taught the three classes differently, in ways specified by the CL matching model *without any knowledge of the model or the nature of the groups*! They simply "read" the students, and let their implicit theories do the rest (Hunt, 1966a).

Although the CL model seemed a potentially useful blueprint, I felt that any psychological theory should be modified on the basis of negative evidence. Have you ever considered how awkward it is for a theorist to change a developmental stage theory? Imagine Larry Kohlberg announcing that Stage 3 actually comes *after* Stage 4 or Erik Erikson changing his "Eight Stages of Man" by reversing two stages—not easy! This was my dilemma when longitudinal evidence and experiments (Wolfe, 1963) showed that what we had called Stage II in 1961 was actually a mixture of two stages that needed to be distinguished. I met this awkward problem with an equally awkward solution: I invented a new stage preceding Stage I, called it "Sub-I," and distinguished it from Stage II. CL theory may be the only example of a stage theory that changed on the basis of research evidence, but I must say I am not very proud of the resulting change. (Who wants to be labeled a Sub-I? In fact, who wants to be called a Stage-anything?)

## Characterization of Upward Bound (1966–1968)

One of my most exciting assignments in those days was to direct the national evaluation of Project Upward Bound, a "Head Start for teenagers." From 1966 to 1968, I conducted the characterization (a term I preferred to evaluation) of projects that comprised over 200 individual programs sponsored by the Office of Economic Opportunity. Most of these programs were associated with universities or colleges where summer programs were held; they served more than 35,000 disadvantaged adolescents each year.

Of my many experiences with Upward Bound, I want to mention two. One shows how a matching model can inform the characterization of program effects. We selected 10% of the programs (21 out of 210) to characterize. The programs selected varied widely in terms of structure as well as the predominant CL of the students in each program. Using these two variables—average student CL and degree of program structure—we placed the 21 programs in categories that could be considered matched or mismatched according to the CL matching model. Low CL-high structure and high CL-low structure were considered "matched" while the opposite combination, low CL-low structure and high CL-high structure, were considered "mismatched." Since we had collected a large number of paper-and-pencil measures before and after the summer program, it was fairly easy to determine matching effects by comparing change scores in the 11 programs that were matched with those in the 10 programs that were not.

The average change score for over 100 students is very imprecise, so while matching effects were logically expected, my hopes for observing them were not very high. Imagine my surprise when we found that the programs structured

# Beginning with Myself

to match the needs of the students produced changes that, compared with the mismatched programs, were significantly greater on several measures [such as attitude to program, motivation for college, perceived possibility of college graduation, and interpersonal flexibility (Hunt & Hardt, 1967)]. On reading our report, the national director asked if the matching-model blueprint should be added to the program guidelines for the following summer so the program directors would formally adjust their program structure to their students. Formalizing the matching prescriptions into guidelines smacked of homogeneous grouping, where matching prescriptions may be used to restrict rather than enhance student development. I was therefore relieved that the new Upward Bound guidelines did not include these formal recommendations. So much for the good news about Upward Bound.

Our first-year characterization results were similar to the pattern of most short-term intervention programs, showing immediate positive effects (measured at the end of the summer program) that extinguish over time (measured the following spring back in their regular school settings). However, our second-year results turned up a more promising picture. In our second year, about one-third of the students had participated in the first year. When we separated the results for these students from those for the first-year students, we found that, when retested in their schools in the spring of their second year, the second-year students did not show the typical decrease. On several measures these students sustained their summer gains. I was excited because we had some "hard data" to support the case for students spending two summers in the program in order to consolidate their gains. I sent a report to this effect to the director of OEO, and I was amazed at his response. He was unequivocally against *any* students repeating the program because 35,000 new students would represent 35,000 new voting families. I am paraphrasing his response in bald form—it came embellished in bureaucratic jargon—but its message was loud and clear. I will never forget this—my first lesson in what happens when research evidence conflicts with political reality.

## Assessment and Training of Training Agents (1965–1967)

While Upward Bound focused on students, several other federal action programs focused on teachers or, more generally, on training agents (e.g., the Teacher Corps and the Peace Corps). I needed a model to work on these programs, so I developed a model for analyzing the training of training agents (Hunt, 1966b). In it I used the three components of Kurt Lewin's classic formula $B$ehavior = $P$erson and $E$nvironment. In this model, teaching is viewed as E:P → B. The teacher provides a teaching approach, or environment (E), for the student (P) in order to produce some outcome (B). The B, P, and E components, which Sullivan and I later used as the basis for *Between Psychology and Education* (Hunt & Sullivan, 1974), defined the necessary skills for a training agent; when combined, they called for more complex skills, such as flexible modulation, or "flexing." When I applied this model to the assessment of Peace Corps trainees and the training of Teacher Corps trainees (Hunt, 1970), I separated this "training agent" work from the matching models (as one might divide teaching from learning). It was not until several years later, following one of Seymour Sarason's stimulating comments, that I began to see how this work fitted into my matching ideas.

What helped me see this connection was a communication task I developed to bring out the processes of "reading" and "flexing" by confronting trainees (communicators) with a role-playing listener who raised obstacles to communication (Hunt, 1970). I had seen all kinds of individual variations up until then, but I had never observed anything to equal the astonishing variation among these communicators as they encountered obstacles. Some seemed completely unaware of the obstacles and "steamrollered" on, some were aware (that is, "read" the obstacles) but had no idea what to do, and others "read" them and changed their way of communicating appropriately ("flexed"). Although the variation was generally apparent, I did not consider it in terms of patterns of "reading" and "flexing" until they were quantitatively verified in factor analysis (Hunt, 1970). I was not prepared to recognize "matching in the moment" (Hunt, 1982a); I still needed "hard data."

The year 1968 brought the most significant event in my professional career: I joined the Department of Applied Psychology at the Ontario Institute for Studies in Education (OISE). Founded in 1965, OISE experienced the expected growing pains of a unique institution, combining a graduate school of education with a large research and development center and field centers. Despite its initial difficulties, it provided an excellent opportunity for me to apply the matching model more intensively and extensively than I ever had before. It was then an ideal place for me to extend the practical value of my theory. It has continued to provide an ideal climate for my development as an applied psychologist; many of my ideas would simply not have emerged had I not come here.

# Application of a Matching Model (1971–1976)

## Matching Models in Education (1971)

I had introduced the idea of matching into the literature in 1961, and ten years later I published *Matching Models in Education* (Hunt, 1971), which brought together my theories and empirical evidence on this topic. My aims were (1) to raise the awareness of practitioners and theorists about the importance of matching and (2) to legitimize the direct application of the CL matching model to educational practice in a variety of settings.

Public education in Ontario had been influenced by the 1968 Hall-Dennis report, which recommended a student-centered approach (just as the Plowden Report in Great Britain had recommended informal approaches in the classroom). Following Hall-Dennis, provincial educational guidelines called for greater student autonomy and less teacher direction. As is usually the case with such sweeping swings of the policy pendulum, teachers and administrators were well aware that these new recommendations might work for some students but would be disastrous for others. Several educational practitioners whose experience told them that different approaches were required for different students were enthusiastic about the prospects of my matching ideas because they legitimized the necessity for a variety of approaches and not simply an unstructured, student-centered approach.

One such advocate was Sam Chapman, Director of Education at the York County Board of Education, a remarkable educator who is on my short list of heroes in education. The fortunate match between practitioner Chapman and theorist Hunt can be seen in his 1971 comment: "Students need different types of learning environments and the considered deliberate provision of suitable environments is more vital to the individualization of education than that of the frenzied changes in administrative practices and course offerings to which we now devote so much energy" (Chapman, 1971a, p. 16).

Sam Chapman's enthusiastic reaction to my matching ideas made possible my work at Thornlea Secondary School and with the Twinning Project. My good fortune in having the endorsement of this perceptive man can be seen in his concluding comments to me in a letter of July 10, 1971: "I've had a gut feeling for years that there is a much better way of deciding what kind of approach we should be using for various students, and your work is the first evidence that has crept into my rather limited world to give me hope that this could be done" (Chapman, 1971b). Even Kurt Lewin couldn't have wished for a better opening to show the practicality of his theory—so here we go.

## Thornlea Characterization Project (1971–1976)

Inspired by Sam Chapman and his colleagues, the Thornlea Secondary School opened in 1968. It was a school of its time, dedicated to teaching students to direct their own learning. During the early 1970s I initiated a five-year longitudinal study, the Thornlea Characterization Project. Unlike some later projects, this one did not provide formal guides for matching (e.g., homogeneous groups). Since the major objective at Thornlea—to foster student independence and self-direction—agreed so closely with the values of the CL developmental theory in which autonomy and self-direction were qualities of the highest stage, I was asked to conduct this study as a means of characterizing how well school objectives were being met.

As shown in Figure 2–1, the major results of the five-year study (Hunt, 1975) showed an increase in student self-direction. Although linking this growth directly with the influence of Thornlea was not possible, these quantitative results, when combined with interviews and our observations, were quite compelling. Thornlea critics could say that the students might have developed autonomy without Thornlea, but to most this possibility seemed unlikely.

**Figure 2–1**

**Thornlea Student CL Scores Over 5 Years**

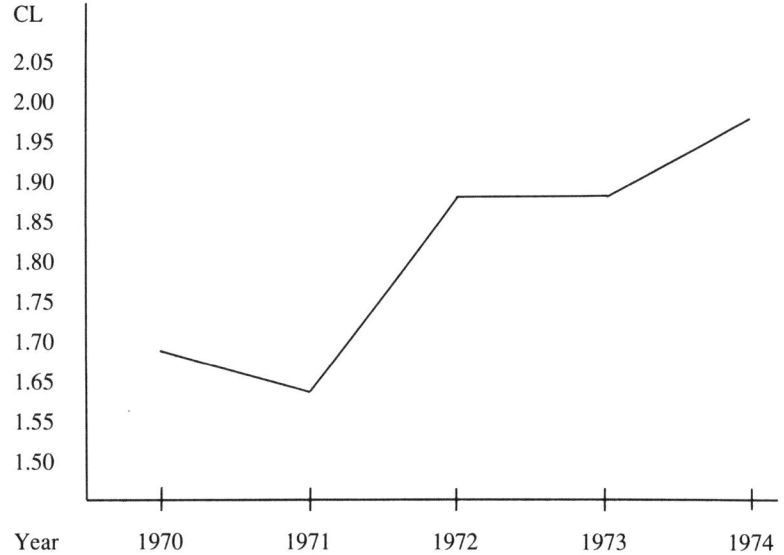

## Beginning with Myself

My most indelible learning at Thornlea took place in 1972 when I actually taught some real students. (I hope my graduate students will forgive me here—they are real too; but you know what I mean.) I co-taught three classes in a ninth-grade course, "Man and Society," which was really a bootleg introduction to psychology. After writing in an abstract way about "radiating certain environments" and "modulating from one environment to another," this first-hand immersion in day-to-day classroom work was very humbling and extremely valuable. As I taught the same topic to the three classes, I was bewildered to find that one day my first class might sparkle while the second fell flat and that the next day the opposite might be true. This brief teaching stint not only opened my eyes to the overwhelming complexity of the classroom but also gave me a teacher's-eye view, and made me understand why most teachers pay attention only to those experts with actual classroom experience—others need not apply.

In observing other classes, I also found that, contrary to Thornlea's image as a place to "do your own thing," the students and teachers there ran the gamut of learning styles and teaching approaches. If appropriate, courses and classes were taught in a structured, teacher-centered fashion. After five years, I saw that Thornlea was not a monolithic permissive oasis; it offered a range of teaching approaches in which teachers were extremely conscientious about each student, dependent or independent, and taught accordingly. I came to believe that it was this caring on the part of so many teachers that created the climate of personalization that made Thornlea so special.

I also learned a great deal about longitudinal research that is not in the methodology books. Working intensively for a long period of time with the same people highlights the participants' perceptions of the researcher's role. How they understood my intentions about characterizing their school was crucial in how they responded to the questionnaires and interviews. What was my role title in the school? One of the teachers came up with the delightfully ambiguous title "resident-visitor," which seemed fine. Was I a friend and supporter of Thornlea? Since I spent one or two days a week there in addition to my teaching stint, I seemed to be on its side. Not very scientific, but had I played the "white-coated scientist" in testing and interviewing them, I am convinced that the students would have resisted cooperation, either actively by refusing to participate or passively by responding in an offhand manner.

In administering the same paper-and-pencil tests year after year (as required in longitudinal research), I learned that there is nothing high school students dislike more than having to respond to the *same* test, even at one-year intervals. Test experts may think that test-retest reliability is the most important criterion (shades of my master's thesis!), but I wonder if they have considered the attitudes of the respondents when asked to take it again. To deal with their resistance, I met with all the 200-plus students in small groups to explain the difference between longitudinal and cross-sectional research, and why it was essential to proceed with longitudinal research, which required their annual cooperation for us to obtain accurate information about their experience at Thornlea. My approach was not scientific and is not in the research method books, but it was absolutely essential for maintaining the good will of the participants.

I was very grateful to the Thornlea students for their candor and openness, both in my classes and on the research project. Partly because of the open atmosphere of the school, Thornlea students asked questions and raised issues that students in other schools would have thought but not felt free to bring up. They did not tolerate fools gladly: Why do we have to do this? Who's going to get your report? How do you know this test measures independence? And, most of all, what will I as a student get out of this project? I answered the last question by promising reports to each of them and individual feedback sessions at the end of the study. In responding to their questions, I realized the need for such a project to be planned collaboratively with the staff and students so that they do not see themselves as passive subjects.

Having established Thornlea's image as a progressive alternative providing less structure for students who were more self-directed, Sam Chapman's next step was to initiate a structured school, which I describe in the following section.

## Twinning Program (1972 – 1974)

In the autumn of 1972, Aurora High School opened as a more structured York County alternative to Thornlea. Newspaper stories about the school bore such headlines as "York County Educator Attempts to Design a New Old-Fashioned School" and "New Strict School Gives Parents More Choice"; some compared Aurora to Thornlea as "Hard School versus Soft School." (Because Aurora was 15 miles north of Thornlea, the two schools were ideological rather than actual alternatives.)

Aurora High School differed from most schools in the early 1970s in at least two respects: in its philosophy of structure and knowledge-centered approach and in the clarity of its mandate to develop a school environment that would be consistent with these values. It was also to feature clear expectations and standards, especially appropriate for students requiring high structure. As you may have noticed, the not-so-subtle influence of the CL matching model was the blueprint for Aurora.

Principal and staff were selected on the basis of this particular belief in education (unusual in a public high school), and the early days went well. Had Aurora continued as Thornlea did—as an alternative to all other York County schools—or had it been possible to "twin" it with Thornlea to provide a distinct alternative, the next few years might have gone more smoothly. What actually happened was that the Board decided to twin the new Aurora High School with the 25-year-old G.W. Williams Secondary School because Williams was only one mile away. Thus, with very little warning and no consultation, the principal and 87 teachers at Williams, who had been serving all types of students in a composite school for years, suddenly found themselves designated as the other half of the Twinning Project with Aurora. The two schools were to share a common attendance area, and incoming eighth-grade students would choose one of the two on the basis of student learning style or need for structure.

The Twinning Project began on the assumption that the two schools would provide two distinctly different environments. This came as news to the Williams staff. Not only was there no consultation but also there was no in-service training to prepare them to serve students needing little structure. On the Williams side at least, the Twinning Project left much to be desired. For me, it was not only another rude awakening to the world of expedient and political reality, it also gave new meaning to the phrase "non-events" (Charters & Jones, 1973).

Although it seemed to some at the time that all of the planning for the Twinning Project was based on CL matching theory, it was only a general guide and certainly did not account for including Williams. My main responsibility was the modest task of helping the eighth-grade students and their parents choose the school that would best reflect the student's learning style. After spending considerable time assessing several hundred students, giving individual feedback, consulting with teachers, and meeting with parents to explain the rationale for the Twinning Program—how it was designed to meet specific student learning needs—I learned a great deal about the gap between theory and real life. The parents were asked to decide, with their children, which learning style would be most appropriate. After these information sessions, they inevitably expressed their gratitude for my help and asked, "Dr. Hunt, which school is better?" It seemed that most parents did not base their school preference on their child's learning style but on whether it agreed with their own educational values.

I must say that sometimes when I met with individual students in feedback sessions I was impressed with their accurate self-assessment of their need for structure (as compared with results from the CL test), but when it came to school choice, it was another story. A student, well aware of the need for considerable structure, would select the less structured school. When asked why, he would reply, "I think it will be a challenge." I eventually learned to translate this statement into "That's where my girlfriend is going." Learning style was definitely a minor factor in school choice. Parents were primarily concerned with selecting the school that agreed with their own philosophy of education, while students were concerned with being with their friends. Both were concerned with which school was closer to home. I did not abandon my ideas for educational alternatives, but I certainly revised them in light of this experience.

## Homogeneous Classroom Grouping by Learning Style (1971–1976)

During this period I was also working on the application of the CL matching model at the classroom level in several North York junior high schools. In contrast to my York County work, the request to use the model came from the teachers and not the director, the unit was not a school but a single classroom, and the planning was more collaborative.

These collaborative projects typically developed from an arrangement in which several teachers working as a team were responsible for organizing several classes of students in whatever way they wished. For example, an early request came from four teachers—English, math, science, and social science—responsible for approximately 120 ninth-grade students in a "house" structure with a large block of time each day to be organized. These teachers had observed that their students displayed very different ways of learning, ways that seemed to be distinguishable from academic ability, and they invited me to talk to them about my matching model. I agreed to assess their students on the CL measure and to form four classes, each of which would be homogenous in need for structure. Since I did not want to create ability groups in disguise, I insisted that the formation of the CL groups also take academic ability into account so the four groups would be roughly equated on ability but would differ in need for structure. The teachers also agreed that student development—increasing self-direction—was a goal for every student in every group. This collaboration would not have been possible without their principal, Ron Wilson, another of my heroes in education who has taught me a great deal about schools.

I worked with teachers in five different schools during the next six years in much the same way, always at the teachers' invitation and always explaining the work to the students and their parents. Because I had become quite conscious of the fact that CL, or degree of need for structure, is only one of numerous dimensions of learning style, I was relieved to observe that teachers quickly and intuitively adapted to the many other student needs. It seemed that grouping by need for structure made this characteristic so explicit that the teachers were then free to concentrate on other areas of student variation.

These projects were enormously complex, but I came to realize that when they produced improved learning environments it was mainly due to the very competent and conscientious teachers. More specifically, I came to see that the homogeneous grouping, whether an effective educational device or not, was very valuable for increasing teachers' awareness by confronting them with the need to adapt to approaching very different classes in very different ways. Although I am not necessarily an advocate of homogeneous grouping (for reasons described earlier in this chapter under *Matching Through Homogeneous Grouping* ), it may serve this unexpected purpose when used temporarily. I was pleased when, after teaching homogeneous classes for one year, the teachers decided to return to mixed classes but requested learning-style information about their students that could be incorporated into their heterogeneous classes.

There were three important differences between this experience with homogeneous grouping and that ten years earlier in Syracuse: (1) teachers were full collaborators in planning, evaluating, and modifying the program; (2) teachers were encouraged to consider student differences other than need for structure in adapting their approaches; and (3) students' initial CL or need for structure was viewed as a starting point to help students become more self-directed and independent.

# There Is Nothing So Theoretical as Good Practice (1976 – Present)

The best way to introduce this last phase is to describe how I reversed my thinking: reversing stingers, turning phrases around, turning ideas upside-down. Why I did this is hard to say—boredom, relief from hardening of the categories, hidden sub-personalities—who knows? I summarize the rationale later, but I really don't believe it was a very rational process. I have noticed that in the relatively infrequent cases in which psychological theorists, myself included, change their theories, they are more likely to do so because they have grown tired of their old ideas than because of logic or experimental evidence. This observation, which some find shocking, is further evidence for Inside-out.

Let me begin with Table 2–1 (see overleaf) by listing a number of stingers and concepts in their original form and then in their reversed form to show how I was thinking.

I am indebted to Richard de Charms for the body-mind reversal: His three-month visit to OISE in 1976 was very stimulating. (We collaborated on a piece, "There Is Nothing So Theoretical as Good Practice," which encountered strong resistance from Outside-in and was never published.)

**Table 2-1**

| Original Form | Reversed Form |
|---|---|
| There is nothing so practical as a good theory. | There is nothing so theoretical as good practice. |
| Theory → practice | Practice → theory |
| Practice makes perfect | Practice makes theory |
| Practice what you preach | Preach what you practice |
| Teacher → student | Student → teacher |
| Mind → body | Body → mind |

The list in Table 2-1 is quite incomplete in that it should contain a final column showing reciprocal relationships between each pair.

| One-way | Reversed One-way | Reciprocal |
|---|---|---|
| Teacher → Student | Student → Teacher | Student ↔ Teacher |

In this example, the reversed claim that students influence teachers (i.e., "student pull") is as one-sided and incomplete as the original claim that teachers influence students. I use reversal to call attention to its original one-sidedness. The ultimate aim is to portray a reciprocal, two-way relationship, e.g., Body ↔ Mind. I will try to show the value of viewing parts in relation to one another, whether these parts of the whole are abstractions, such as Practice ↔ Theory, or persons, such as Consultant ↔ Teacher. I hope to communicate reciprocal relationships in a concrete way because, although they seem abstract and complex, I believe that reciprocality is the fundamental ingredient in human affairs.

## Teachers Are Psychologists, Too (Hunt, 1976a)

The subtitle of "Teachers Are Psychologists, Too"—"On the Application of Psychology to Education,"—illustrates my reshaping of ideas about the relationship between practice and theory at this time. In this paper, I traced my first awareness of the need to "begin with the teacher" to a 1971 quotation from *Matching Models in Education* (Hunt, 1971):

> Assuming that the matching principle is sufficiently well established, it seems probable that one of the major determinants of its acceptability will be the degree to which it is congruent with the teacher's ideas of matching. If so, then the task of implementing a matching model should begin with an investigation of what implicit matching model the educational decision maker is now using. (p. 49)

Looking at this 1971 quote makes me wonder if I ever read what I write. Anyway, the seed for Inside-out was there, though couched in Outside-in (implementation) language. To bring out "the teacher's own ideas of matching" was precisely what I had in mind when I dusted off the old Kelly Rep Test in 1974 and began to develop what became "How To Be Your Own Best Theorist" (Hunt, 1980a), as described in Chapter 4.

## Teacher's Adaptation: "Reading" and "Flexing" to Students (Hunt, 1976b)

This paper made the case for "reading" and "flexing" by focusing on student pull (student → teacher). Noting that compared with thousands of studies investigating how teachers influence students, only a handful study how students influence teachers, I outlined a way in which we might reverse this process in designing experiments. Student reaction would be systematically varied through their verbal or non-verbal behavior to observe how teachers would respond. I was less interested in convincing readers to design experiments of student pull than I was in giving concrete meaning to "reading" and "flexing," which would be required in order for teachers to respond.

## Theory-to-Practice as Persons-in-Relation (Hunt, 1977b)

I borrowed the phrase "persons-in-relation" from the philosopher John MacMurray (1961) and began to recast practice-theory relationships accordingly, as discussed in detail in Chapter 7. For now, let me summarize this piece in Figure 2-2.

## Figure 2-2
## Traditional and "Persons-in-Relation" View of Theory-Practice

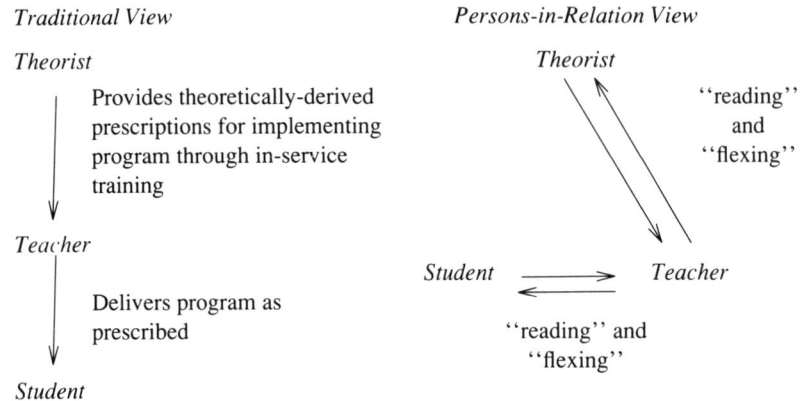

*Source*: Hunt, 1977b

I clarified the difference in the two views by using the CL matching model in my work with teachers:

> ... I suddenly realized that the CL matching principle was not what was accounting for the major effect. ... What was making the difference was an underlying process of interpersonal communication, or more specifically, a communicator's "reading" and "flexing" to a listener. In my work with the teachers I tried to "read" their conceptions and "flex" to them, e.g., translating CL to learning style. I did this unselfconsciously, but I now realize that my concrete interactions with the teachers (how we were as persons-in-relation) exemplified how I hoped they would interact with their students. (Hunt, 1977b, p. 54–55)

## Theorists Are Persons, Too (Hunt, 1978a)

This paper, which extended the ideas in the preceding paper, is less important for what it said than for the reaction it provoked, which was my first experience with mainstream psychology's resistance to an Inside-out approach. The following comment, written, oddly enough, by a friend of mine, appeared in a review of the book in which my paper was published.

Hunt's prescription is that theorist, practitioner and client can only influence each other by interacting in the actual program. ... This is a strange position for one of the co-authors of Harvey, Hunt and Schroder's influential work on personality development to find himself in, and he seems to be overminimizing the advantages that a practitioner can derive from a knowledge of theories of personality functioning and development. (Taft, 1979, p. 24)

With friends like this. . . .

## From Single Variable to Persons-in-Relation (Hunt, 1980b)

I include "From Single Variable to Persons-in-Relation" here because its title conveys both the incompleteness of such single variables as CL and the necessity for building an understanding of persons-in-relation on a *complete* version of a person. That I simply found CL, like any other psychological characteristic, to be insufficient and therefore unsatisfactory for a persons-in-relation account (Hunt, 1983a) is the only rational means I have found for explaining to other psychological researchers who accuse me of abandoning it.

# Overcoming Resistance from Inside and Outside

I conclude this chapter with a description of the obstacles I have experienced to adopting an Inside-out approach and how I have tried to overcome them. First, however, two points must be made clear. My emphasis on the value of Inside-out does not mean that I propose to abandon Outside-in altogether. As I described earlier, these two concepts operate in reciprocal relation to one another. I could not have begun as a psychologist by relying only on what was Inside because it was necessary to take in from the Outside first. I therefore emphasize that my recommendations are directed to *experienced* practitioners, who, it must be remembered, can also profit from Outside-in but only *after* consolidating their own Inside areas. Self-knowledge precedes learning from others. For practitioners-in-training, more Outside-in is probably required.

Second, I want to distinguish Inside-out from "going public" with your ideas; the latter leads to a source of internal resistance. In considering an Inside-out approach, I hope that you will consider it fundamentally as a process of bringing out your implicit ideas and beliefs *to yourself*. Inside-out does not require bringing out your unexpressed ideas for all to see—not at all. Rather, to realize that you own your ideas increases your own agency and control, which creates more choices. One way to remain private is to keep a journal in which you make your thoughts and ideas explicit to yourself. These thoughts are yours to do with as you will. You may decide to share them or to discuss them with colleagues, but this is a choice you can make later, and you may decide to "go public" with some and not with others. When I use exercises to facilitate Inside-out, I do not always maintain a strict line between identifying self-knowledge and sharing it, but I do try and I hope you clearly understand this distinction.

## Inside Obstacles and Overcoming Them

I devoted a great deal of time and energy on my last sabbatical in the spring of 1980 to personal development and self-awareness. I think it helped me learn more about my internal resistance to Inside-out. I was very lucky to have my good friend John Weiser introduce me to guided imagery and sub-personalities. As John knows, I was much less interested in the theory of psychosynthesis, on which these ideas are based, than in my experience with them. (I had heard more than enough theory at that point.)

The concept of sub-personalities implies that we have many parts of ourselves, like my Little Professor and Little Optimist. Some are strongly in evidence and others are dormant and undeveloped. This simple idea—that each of us has many parts and that we are more than the sum of these parts—came to me, both as a sometime psychological theorist and to my inner being, as a stunning revelation. My Professor Theorist was flabbergasted at the implications of the single-dimensional personality theories of mainstream psychology when viewed in terms of sub-personalities. To take one small example, what happens to the test-retest reliability of a personality measure if the respondent takes the initial test from the perspective of one sub-personality (e.g., the conforming part) but takes the retest from the perspective of another (e.g., the rebellious part)? You can easily see that there would not be much left of traditional personality theory and measurement if we were to acknowledge the operation of sub-personalities.

I was, however, not really concerned with the future of mainstream personality theory. What stirred my inner being was that I was immediately able to recognize part of my personal cast of sub-personalities and, equally important, saw that some seemed to be missing, causing me to try to coax them out on stage. After John Weiser's introduction, I began to work on my own by writing a morning review of the preceding day, directing myself in guided imagery that in turn brought out certain sub-personalities, representing, among other aspects, mind, body, and feelings.

## Beginning with Myself

At the time I was in the midst of an exciting but puzzling attempt to begin with myself and could not then have seen my experience as clearly as I do now. I identified the major obstacles to be my overwhelmingly analytical mind (which I sometimes symbolized as a metallic Big Wheel with cogs) and the undeveloped state of my feelings and emotions (sometimes symbolized as a Fairy Princess). My earlier reference to the form of poetry called Haiku in examples of stingers was because I found writing in its 17-syllable form valuable in consolidating and expressing the awareness I had gained in my sub-personality work. My 17-syllable "stingers in verse" were certainly not Haiku in other respects—my only criterion for this doggerel was that it contain 17 syllables. I certainly did not intend to "go public" with these verses, but I share a few of them here because they express my struggle in going Inside-out. I present them in pairs—first the obstacle and then the overcoming of it.

> Clinking - clanking, creaking - cracking,
> Big Wheel Robot
> Screech - grinds to a halt

> Flashing silver glitter,
> Fairy Princess
> Turns Robot to Shining Knight

And later:

> When I am not open,
> Quicksilver feelings
> Harden to Big Wheel Steel

> When I am open,
> Big Wheel dissolves
> To a circle of my whole self.

Still later, working on bringing my parts together:

> A ticket to ride
> On the Ferris Wheel
> It starts, and all of us fly

> Rolling round and round,
> Tinkling tiny tendrils
> Play a Song in my Heart

> Taking the magic wand
> From my feelings
> I run the relay anchor

## Outside Obstacles and Overcoming Them

External resistance to my becoming an Inside-out psychologist has been illustrated by the reviewer's rejection of my proposing that "theorists are persons, too" and by academic visitors who view my development as abandoning CL theory and Outside-in. A final example occurred in the spring of 1983 when I presented a paper at an AERA (American Educational Research Association) meeting in Montreal as part of a symposium on learning style. My paper (Hunt, 1983b) described the Inside-out approach used in a workshop, Identifying Your Own Learning Style, and *made absolutely no reference whatsoever to my earlier work on the CL matching model.* Two discussants, who had both read my paper and heard what I said, commented extensively on my CL matching model but made absolutely no reference to my Inside-out paper! That is resistance.

My response to this resistance from mainstream psychology and the educational research establishment is found in Chapter 6, where I address it directly. I have few illusions about changing these Outside-in institutions, though I hope some theorists and researchers will cut through this resistance.

At a less grandiose level, I have dealt with external resistance by creating an informal support group of colleagues. Several years ago I initiated an informal bi-weekly discussion group of colleagues interested in staff development. One of my purposes was to bring colleagues who work in professional development with elementary and secondary school teachers together with others who work with college and university teachers. Our luncheon discussion meetings sometimes have a theme but are often unplanned. Since all of the participants are actively engaged in educational development, the discussions are almost always based on recent examples, which give an immediate vibrancy to them. I find this group of congenial colleagues an excellent antidote to external constraints and hardening of the categories. Our group gatherings are in the spirit of the original teacher centers in Great Britain—they are informal, voluntary, grass roots, practical, and fun.

In describing my stepping stones as well as in mentioning other approaches such as journal keeping and sub-personality work, I have tried to illustrate the spirit of beginning with ourselves. In addition to these tools which you may wish to try, I describe several other tools for beginning with ourselves in the following chapters.

# 3
# Beginning with Ourselves in Learning Style

## How Are We Alike and How Are We Different?

One of my favorite stingers is the introductory statement in Kluckhohn and Murray's 1949 book, *Personality*:

> Every person is like *every* other person in some ways,
> Every person is like *some* other person in some ways,
> Every person is like *no* other person in some ways. (p. 1)

A little long for a stinger maybe, but it carries much wisdom. Each of us is like every one of the five billion other persons as we are all human, yet each of us is also unique in our distinctive combination of human qualities. This stinger can be transformed by substituting "student," "client," or "teacher" for "person." Better still, substitute "I am" for "Every person is" and see what happens. This 30-word stinger captures the dilemma of diversity that we all face, both personally and professionally.

In our everyday lives we deal with such questions as: How can I communicate with this person? How can I help this person? How can I persuade this person? In each case we form an impression, whether we are aware of it or not, that guides our actions in trying to communicate, help, or persuade. We go about these everyday activities not only unaware of how we are forming our impressions, but also usually lacking the self-knowledge required to assess the other person as alike or different from ourselves. We do not usually take an Inside-out approach to bring out our implicit theories of how persons differ. Although we have thousands of specific experiences in dealing with individuality, we are not aware of what we know about it and are likely to feel inadequate—consequently, we seek expert advice about diversity from Outside-in. What does research tell us about the major ways in which people differ?

Practitioners are also caught in the dilemma of coping with diversity. Teachers must form impressions of their students in order to work with the entire class ("Every student is like every other student in some ways"), to work with them in groups ("Every student is like some other student in some ways"), and, when time and circumstance permit, to work with them individually ("Every student is like no other student in some ways"). Consultants form impressions of teachers and supervisors of trainees in the same way.

Most of us are likely to feel overwhelmed at times in our personal and professional lives as we struggle to understand our own individuality and that of others. Note how many of the following questions have occurred to you: What are the most important dimensions in which my students (clients) vary? What consulting approach will work for most of my clients? How can I quickly assess my clients in terms of their major distinctive dimensions? Which individual characteristics are likely to develop and which are not? Which one should I try to change? In addition to questions concerning diversity in others, we want to understand ourselves: How are we alike and how are we different from others? How much can we change? Do we work best with people similar or different from ourselves?

No wonder psychologists have been busy trying to answer these questions from their theories and research. They have applied many names to their work over the years—individual differences, personality variation, aptitudes, and so on. This topic, individuality in human affairs, provides an ideal example to show how it may be approached from Inside-out as well as from Outside-in and to show how the two approaches may be combined. The most recent entry in the individuality sweepstakes has been *learning style,* and I use this idea to organize this chapter, first describing it briefly and then discussing the ways in which it can be approached both Inside-out and Outside-in.

*Beginning with Ourselves in Learning Style*

# What is Learning Style?

W.C. Fields' stinger that "Style is everything" may be a little strong but in the 1980s style is certainly "in." In addition to learning styles, there are teaching styles, communication styles, cognitive styles, work styles, management styles, supervisory styles, and, of course, life styles. If you want to describe individual variations in any area, simply add the word "styles."

Learning style is synonymous with communication style in its attempt to characterize how a person receives and transmits information. In the next section, I show how, from an Inside-out view, learning style systematizes our fleeting impressions of others as we communicate with them. I try to anchor your understanding of learning style firmly in your own direct experience because the Outside-in approach to learning style is complex and mystifying.

Many Outside-in learning style models have sprung up since 1970, and they come in a variety of sizes (from 1 to 28 dimensions), shapes (quadrants, graphs, psychographs, circles), and kinds (systematic-intuitive, visual-auditory, right brain-left brain). Also, each model has its own specific questionnaire to be used in assessment. Small wonder that most practitioners are overwhelmed and confused by these complex schemes.

Like any Outside-in approach, these models, or portions of them, may have value for practitioners, but first practitioners must reclaim their experienced knowledge, which is the purpose of the next two sections on learning style Inside-out.

# Matching in the Moment

In this section you are asked to reflect briefly on your experience to bring out what you know, but may not have identified, about informally assessing the learning style of others as you communicate with them and about matching your communication with this informal assessment. Becoming aware of your own "matching in the moment" is the first step in demystifying the idea of learning style. Going Inside-out to bring out your awareness of matching in the moment provides you with a personal foundation from which to consider the Outside-in information discussed later. The following description of matching in the moment is an excerpt from "The Practical Value of Learning Style Ideas" (Hunt, 1982a).

Learning style is nothing more than a formal attempt to capture what goes on in effective communication. Learning style ideas attempt to make part of the teaching-learning and counseling transactions explicit—an explication practitioners themselves are much too busy to bring to consciousness, let alone describe in detail.

Our first step, therefore, is to get a feeling for this intuitive, implicit process which makes interpersonal communication possible, yet usually passes without notice. To get a first-hand understanding of this process, I ask you to reflect on what goes through your mind when you are communicating with another person.

Stop for another moment and imagine yourself in the following situation: As you are leaving work, you are stopped outside by a foreign visitor who inquires, in barely understandable English, how to find the nearest railroad station. What goes through your mind? Do you ask any questions before you reply to the request? What is your initial impression of the visitor?

Suppose further that the visitor does not understand your initial attempt at directions. What do you do next? Focus on your train of thought throughout all of this interchange. Notwithstanding the limitations of hypothetical situations, I hope that your reflection led you to a sharper awareness of certain identifiable processes in your experience.

How does the following two-step sequence fit with your analysis? An initial attempt is made to form an impression of the visitor (perhaps accompanied by a question or two to verify your impression), which in turn forms the basis for adapting your response to his request. Does it make sense to think of this interchange as two steps involving "reading" and "flexing" (Hunt, 1976b) in which you form an impression and then act on this impression?

We cannot be this reflective, of course, in the moment when the split-second demands of the situation collapse this reading and flexing into the indistinguishable flow of conversational give and take. Reading and flexing are like perception and action, one leading to, or occurring simultaneously with, the other.

These two steps may also be viewed as "if . . . then" matching statements. We form a hunch about the other person in terms of "If this person is thus-and- so," which leads to an action statement, "then I should approach the person this way." You might have formed the impression, for instance, that a visitor would be familiar with maps, and therefore decided to draw instructions for him to find a place. It is very unlikely that in this case you have gone through "if . . . then" formally by specifying that "*If* he knows about maps, *then* I will respond to his request with instructions on a map." What is more likely is that you formed an implicit hunch about the visitor which affected your way of responding.

I want you to become aware of this intuitive matching process because it is what learning style ideas help us to understand. Assuming that our response of drawing a map for the visitor is based on implicit matching, it is

*Beginning with Ourselves in Learning Style* 41

> very similar to a formal matching prescription such as "If a person experiences events spatially, then I will use maps, globes, and atlases to communicate." Formal matching statements like this, in which the learning style description of spatial orientation serves to guide actions, are valuable because they make the matching process explicit, and therefore communicable. Indeed, the idea of learning style is important because it forms matching statements of the "if . . . then" variety and thereby clarifies what happens in reading and flexing. (Hunt, 1982, pp. 87–88)

Now, with this common-sense version of matching in mind, let us take a look at how this Inside-out approach can be amplified. The following excerpt is taken from "Demystifying Learning Style" (Hunt, 1985).

# Identifying Your Own Learning Style

During the past two years I have worked with several thousand teachers and other practitioners in an experiential workshop, "Identifying Your Own Learning Style." Just as the value gained in an experiential workshop depends on the good will of the participants, the understanding that you, as a reader, will gain from reading about it on these printed pages will depend on your imagining yourself in the workshop and trying some of the exercises.

Chart 1 summarizes three ways to identify learning style, and this workshop focuses on personal experience as a source of understanding and identifying learning styles.

### Chart 1

#### Three Ways to Identify Learning Styles

1. **Theory** — Can it be logically derived?
2. **Research** — Can it be proven experimentally?
3. **Personal Experience** — Does it fit with my experience?

There is nothing wrong with using theory and research to identify learning styles, but I believe that theory- and research-based information will mean more if you begin with yourself. The reasons for this are shown in Chart 2:

## Chart 2

### Why Begin with Teachers' Learning Style?

1. Awareness of your learning style helps you become aware of the styles of your students
2. Your learning style is closely related to your preferred teaching style
3. Understanding your own learning/teaching style helps you identify your own matching models

The workshop aims are (1) to help you to identify your own learning style through a series of exercises and through raising your awareness of how you respond to different learning environments, and (2) to illustrate three different ways in which you might identify the learning styles of your students or clients.

**If You Want to Know, Ask 'Em:** This approach comes from my earlier work with George Kelly who, when he was supervising our clinical training practice made a simple suggestion. "Always ask the client what is wrong, he might tell you." In this approach, you are asked first to think about past experiences in learning—about your work, a hobby, a skill, or whatever—and pick out one which was a good learning experience. Reviewing this particular positive experience in your mind, consider what made it a good experience, and then write down this characteristic in a word or phrase. Next, repeat the same procedure for a negative, or poor, learning experience, jotting down what made it a poor experience. Next, look back at what you observed about the two contrasting experiences, and see if you can go further in identifying the most important difference in the two. Next, you respond to two or three other items such as, "The best way for me to learn . . .", "I have trouble learning when. . . ." Finally, you review what you have written with an eye toward summarizing what, for you, are the most important characteristics, or features, in a learning experience. When these have been summarized then we look at Chart 3.

Chart 3 (see facing page) shows a few dimensions of learning style which have been identified through theory and research. Looking at this chart, see if you can find any of those dimensions you identified through your own personal experience. Also, you might think about whether you would have preferred to see Chart 3 before beginning this exercise since this provides an "experiment" to consider your own style.

**If You Want to Know, Test 'Em:** Most learning style inventories are developed by selecting one or more of the dimensions in Chart 3, and devising questions which will classify the respondent on those specific dimensions. In this workshop I use the Kolb Learning Style Inventory (1976) which is based on the two dimensions—concrete-abstract and active-reflective—as shown in Chart 4 (see facing page).

# Beginning with Ourselves in Learning Style

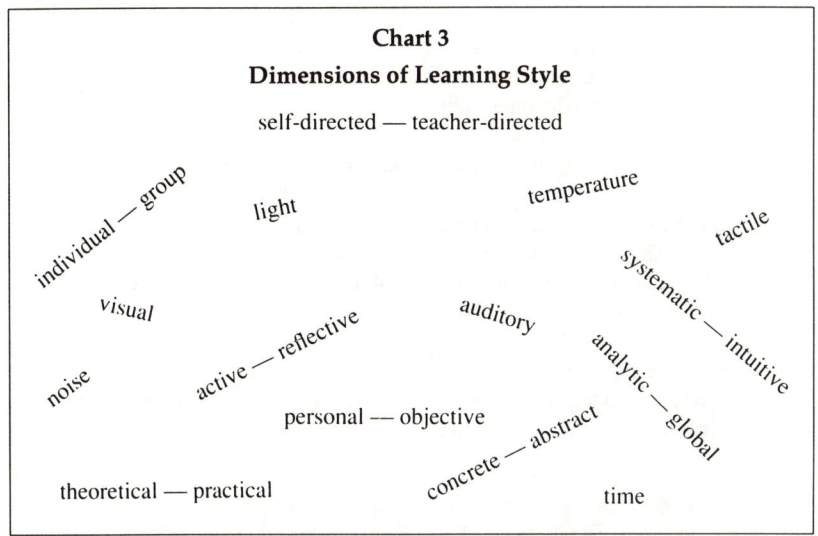

Before taking the test, I would like for you to get an idea of these two dimensions so that you can make your self-assessment as accurate as possible. First consider the vertical concrete-abstract dimensions by reading these descriptions of the two poles (from Kolb, 1976, p. 5):

> *Concrete Experience* (CE): a receptive, experience-based approach relying heavily on feeling-based judgments. Emphasis on specific examples in which each situation can be considered for its unique features. Feedback and discussion with other learners.

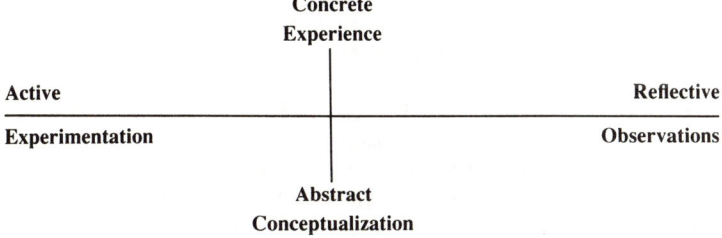

*Abstract Conceptualization* (AC): analytical, conceptual approach relying heavily on logical thinking and rational evaluation. Emphasis on theory and systematic analysis, often in impersonal learning situations.

After considering the concrete-abstract dimension in Chart 4, you are asked to place an "X" on the vertical line to indicate where you think of yourself generally on this dimension. Here you are judging yourself on the dimension on the basis of your own assessment without using an inventory.

Next, read the descriptions of the poles on the Active-Reflective dimension and make an "X" in this dimension (from Kolb, 1976, p. 5).

*Active Experimentation* (AE): An active "doing" orientation relying heavily on experimentation. Emphasis on engaging in projects, homework, or small group discussion rather than lectures.

*Reflective Observation* (RO): Tentative, impartial reflective approach. Emphasis on careful observation and taking information through impartial, objective observations as in lectures or library.

Finally, put yourself into one of the four quadrants on the basis of your two X's.

Following your "intuitive" self-assessment, you classify yourself into one of the four quadrants using a variation of the Kolb Learning Style Inventory (1976), e.g., "Are you primarily intuitive or logical?" in which you selected between two descriptions (CE vs. AC). When you have recorded your test results with a check, we consider which is most accurate, the X (self-assessment) or the check (test score) to illustrate the test mystique described earlier.

After tallying the number of workshop participants in each of the four quadrants, I ask how many felt uneasy at becoming a single X or check mark, noting that almost every learning style inventory forces the person into a single point on a dimension.

I briefly propose an alternative scheme for characterizing oneself and others on the Kolb model by beginning with the four modes in Chart 4 as part of an experiential learning cycle (as Kolb originally proposed) in which under ideal circumstances, one experiences a sequential cycle CE → RO → AC → AE, and then back to CE again, i.e., we experience something, observe or reflect on it, give it meaning which in turn guides our actions. Viewed as a four-mode cycle rather than four quadrants permits playing a variation on Kolb's theme (Abbey, Hunt, & Weiser, 1985) by considering which of the four modes are well developed in ourselves and which modes undeveloped. Some of us may find that we are well-developed in the upper three modes so that we typically go through a cycle from CE to RO to AE

## Beginning with Ourselves in Learning Style

(eliminating AC) while others may not experience CE, but begin again with RO to AC to AE and back to RO again. The former pattern I call a "Northerner" and the latter a "Southerner" regarding the four points in Chart 4 as compass points. I realize this is a too-brief summary, but I believe this four-mode cycle provides a richer way of thinking about learning style variation, and also seems to provide the basis for characterizing transactions, e.g. imagine the transaction between a teacher who is a "Southerner" and a student who is a "Northerner." (See Chapter 8 for a detailed description.)

**If You Want to Know, Let 'Em Sample the Options:** This is how we can identify our learning style through a direct attempt to use certain approaches and noting their availability and ease. It also illustrates that styles vary in how we receive, hold and send, experience as shown in Chart 5:

**Chart 5**

**Three Types of Learning Styles**

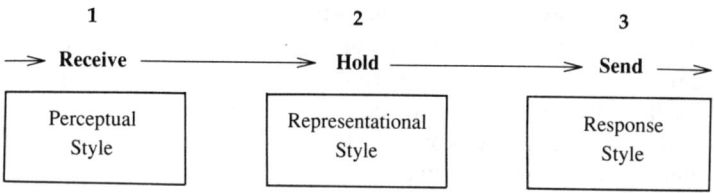

We usually think of variations in modality, e.g. visual and auditory, as referring to how we receive experience. Bandler and Grinder (1979) noted we also differ in how we *represent* experience in our minds, i.e. in visual form as pictures, in auditory form as tapes, or in tactile form as feelings. They have proposed a fairly complex scheme called Neuro Linguistic Programming (NLP) which is based primarily on persons' varying in terms of their representational systems, e.g. visual, auditory, or kinesthetic, referring to one's "lead channel" as that representational system which is most accessible.

The purpose of this exercise was to assess your own representational systems through using your visual, auditory, and tactile system in a guided imagery exercise. You are asked first to imagine visual experiences, then auditory experiences, and finally, kinesthetic experiences. Following this, you consider which ones were easiest (your lead channel), and we discuss how these variations might help "matching in the moment" (Hunt, 1985, pp. 3–4).

Having brought out your implicit ideas about your own learning style and your "matching in the moment," this Inside-out awareness provides a foundation for you to evaluate Outside-in approaches for possible incorporation into your implicit theories. The next two sections briefly summarize two Outside-in approaches: experimental and marketing.

# The Strange Case of the Missing ATIs

The workshop just described emphasized personal experience, but as indicated in Chart 1, there are other ways to identify learning styles, and some researchers believe that experimental research is the *only* way. These researchers conducted hundreds of experiments between 1957 and 1977. Cronbach and Snow (1977), investigated various combinations of learner characteristics (*A*ptitudes) and teaching approaches (*T*reatments) in order to find those that were most effective (*I*nteraction). An example of this Aptitude-Treatment-Interaction (ATI) approach consists of selecting two groups of learners who differ in some way (Aptitude)—e.g., introverts and extroverts—and systematically exposing them to two teaching approaches (Treatment)—e.g., lecture and group discussion—to observe whether one group learns better with one approach than the other (Interaction). ATI is an experimental approach to verify "matching in the moment."

These researchers followed Robert Thorndike's famous dictum "If it exists it can be measured" and its reversal, "If it cannot be measured or experimentally verified, it does not exist." (Remember, I warned you that not all stingers are true.) I describe this ATI work here not because it contributes to our understanding, but to raise your awareness about what research tells us. ATI work illustrates so well what happens when a commonly experienced phenomenon in human affairs—matching in the moment—undergoes rigorous experimentation in the laboratory.

In addition to Thorndike's transformed stinger, these researchers applied very rigorous statistical criteria to what would constitute "better learning." Interaction in ATI meant *statistical* interaction, and when these criteria were applied to these hundreds of studies, very few ATIs were found to exist. I therefore call this work "the strange case of the missing ATIs."

The following statement by Glass (in Wittrock & Wiley, 1970) summarizes the work:

> There is no evidence for an interaction of curriculum treatments and personological variables. I don't know of another statement that has been confirmed so many times and by so many people. (p. 210)

I don't know of any statement by an educational researcher more likely to convince teachers of the irrelevance of educational research to classroom practice. All teachers know through experience that the effect on different students of different ways of teaching varies enormously; to tell teachers otherwise simply eliminates theory-practice communication.

Not all researchers were as cavalier as Glass, some calling his lack of hard data "inconceivable" (Cronbach & Snow, 1968) and "astounding" (Glaser, 1972). Do you wonder that I called my 1974 paper "Person-Environment Interaction; A Challenge Found Wanting Before it was Tried"? My hopes for the educational research establishment ever relinquishing Thorndike's dictum were slight at best, but my Little Optimist was cheered to read Cronbach's (1975) conclusions (even though the paper was his swan song on this topic):

> The special task of the social scientist in each generation is to pin down the contemporary parts. Beyond that, he shares with the humanistic scholar and the artist in the effort to gain insight into contemporary relationships, and to realign the culture's view of man with present realities. To know man as he is is no mean aspiration. (p. 126)

Lee Cronbach, meet George Kelly! Ten years after Cronbach's concluding exhortation, very few researchers from the psychological establishment (the APA) or the educational establishment (the AERA) have followed his advice, presumably because the negative evidence on ATI in Cronbach and Snow's 1977 book of 574 pages far outweighed these three sentences. By a curious coincidence that bewilders me, as the door closed on matching work among the APA/AERA researchers in the early 1970s, it opened wide for another group whose professional affiliations were primarily with either ASCD (Association for Supervision in Curriculum Development) or NASSP (National Association of Secondary School Principals). Those of you who are allergic to acronyms and initials, please bear with me; this, too, will pass.

# The Marketing of Learning Style

Now we leave the stodgy world of traditional research and theory to enter the dazzling new world of *learning style*. Step right up, ladies and gentlemen, and listen to this charismatic inspirational introduction by one of the leading style merchants:

> It's sorta crazy, the kind of world we're living in these last three years, traveling all over the world and talking about learning style and talking about the most exciting thing that could possibly happen in the world—learning! We're not gonna talk about theory today, we're not gonna talk about some professor out of some tower at some university who says, "Hey, I've got a good idea, why don't you do it? ... Any university profs here? Good. Now the hour is late, you and I have a quest ... to save the ship." (Keynote address, East York Board of Education Professional Development Day, 12 November 1982)

How does that grab you? This kind of pitch has bewitched many bothered and bewildered teachers, and other practitioners, who frequently buy tickets to get inside the tent. My reason for calling the developers of these various learning style models "merchants" of learning style stems from their business-oriented approach, their treating practitioners as consumers. Although not true for all learning style models, in most cases practitioners must purchase the learning style questionnaires, pay to have them scored, and pay again to attend workshops on translating test scores and developing prescriptions for action.

I have intentionally caricatured these learning style models in marketing terms to raise your awareness, if not your wariness, about how you approach them. You may well find value in the models and dimensions summarized in Chart 3, but I strongly recommend that you approach them as a skilled practitioner very knowledgeable about learning style and matching from your own experience, and interested in extending your knowledge by transforming or incorporating one of the models into your own implicit theory. I have found Kolb's experiential learning cycle of considerable value and have transformed it in several ways to serve my own purposes. (This is described in Chapter 8.) Having approached Kolb's model with my own implicit theory in place, I modified it in ways appropriate to my concerns. I did not worry about whether it was more valid than Gregorc's model (1982), which is similar to Kolb's in using Concrete-Abstract but uses Random-Systematic rather than Active-Reflective, nor did I worry about whether to use McCarthy's (1982) variation on Kolb, which slices the pie into eight, rather than four, sections, by dividing each quadrant into a left brain-right brain distinction.

I offer some parting advice in the next section on demystifying learning style, but here I want to emphasize that you consider these models in terms of their potential practical value, not in terms of which one is "true." Worrying about whether Kolb, Gregorc, or McCarthy is right will soon lead you back to the unproductive Outside-in of "the strange case of the missing ATIs." I do not propose mindlessness and non-rational choice—quite the contrary. I propose that you proceed from your experienced position, not as an unskilled consumer.

*Beginning with Ourselves in Learning Style* 49

I noted earlier that practitioners do not have their own language, and some of these models provide them with a language, however exotic, with which to communicate their individuality and that of their colleagues and students. For example, in the Myers-Briggs approach (Lawrence, 1982) persons become four letters, such as ISTJ (which stands for Introverted-Sensing-Thinking-Judgment) and ENFP (for Extroverted-Intuitive-Feeling-Perceptual). This scheme of classifying everyone into one of 16 combinations of these four dimensions may strike you as utterly implausible (who wants to be summed up in four letters?), yet this scheme and others like it have found acceptance in many settings. Practitioners are attracted to such schemes, despite their complexity and awkwardness, because they provide at least some way to describe oneself and one's clients. Apparently it is better to be thought of as an ENFP than not to be thought of as anything at all. In providing a language, this scheme and others like it (for instance, Kolb encourages persons to describe themselves as "convergers," "divergers," "assimilators," and "accommodators," according to their position in one of the four quadrants in Chart 4) allow practitioners and clients to legitimize their individuality: "Don't talk to me that way, I'm an ENFP."

What bothers me most about these schemes is that a person becomes a type, and only a type—whether I am a converger, an ENFP, or a CR (Concrete Random), I am diminished to a dot, a point on a graph. This is demeaning to the complexity of the human condition. In Chapter 8 I suggest an alternative to becoming a dot.

My Little Optimist concludes "The Marketing of Learning Style" by suggesting that you review some of the many learning style models in such summaries as Keefe, 1979; NASSP, 1982; and *Theory into Practice* (Hunt & Gow, 1984). Davidman's 1981 paper "Learning Style: The Myth, the Panacea, the Wisdom" is also worthwhile. In my paper "Teachers Are Psychologists, Too" (Hunt, 1976), I criticize "teacher-proof curriculum," which treats teachers as know-nothings who need to learn in a "paint-by-numbers" way. I view experienced practitioners as skilled artisans who may wish to further improve their skilled performance as skilled painters might fine-tune their skill. Try to come up with a metaphor or analogy about how you might incorporate Outside-in information.

The following, concluding section is another excerpt from "Demystifying Learning Style" (Hunt, 1985).

# Demystifying Learning Style

Like earlier proposals for dealing with student individuality, learning style models are based on three myths: (1) the myth of novelty, (2) the myth of unlimited resources, and (3) the myth that science will improve human affairs. After attempting to debunk these myths in the light of practical reality, I describe learning style models more specifically in terms of their reliance on (1) medical mystique, (2) test mystique, and (3) brain mystique—to show how such mystique cuts teachers off from their own expertise and feelings of adequacy, requiring them to depend more on outside experts. Clearing away myth and mystique sets the stage for showing how every teacher, and indeed every person, is a psychologist; in our everyday lives and teaching we have thousands of experiences with learning style and matching models. In this light, learning style models become possible guides, rather than mystical solutions.

## Myths of Learning Style Models and Other Approaches to Student Individuality

**The Myth of Novelty:** In concluding comments of the monograph *Student Learning Styles,* Keefe (1979) asserts:

> Learning style is much more than just another innovation . . . it is a new way of learning and instruction. . . . It is nothing less than revolutionary. (p. 131)

Compare these dazzling comments to those made to me by a teacher after hearing my description of matching according to learning style (I have perpetrated a few of these myths in my time also):

> I was interested in hearing about your learning style theory. I've been doing that for years, but I didn't know there was a theory to it.

Novelty may alleviate boredom at times, but when it comes to theoretical schemes for improving teaching, the myth of novelty tends to alienate teachers from what they already know and are doing. You can decide for yourself whether you prefer a "revolutionary new idea" or one which is close to your own experience. If you prefer the latter, it does not mean that you will not benefit from the idea. The teacher who made the above comment to me was definitely interested in my ideas, but it was for how they amplified what she already knew, not for their mystical revelations.

**The Myth of Unlimited Resources:** I borrow this term from Seymour Sarason (1972), who called attention to how it operates when new settings are created. In classroom practice, this myth consists of a failure to attend to the teacher's available resources, human and otherwise, in recommending proposals. In the first myth, the teacher comments illustrated cutting through

*Beginning with Ourselves in Learning Style* 51

the myth. Here is a teacher comment, made about Piagetian stage proposals, which illustrates a teacher's accepting the myth of unlimited resources:

> Oh, how I wish I could organize and run my class in terms of each student's developmental stage, like they do in Geneva.

What this teacher did not realize was that, even in Geneva, one teacher has limited available resources which have to do for 30-plus students. The myth of unlimited resources is closely related to the next myth.

**The Myth That Science Will Improve Human Affairs:** One of the reasons that proposals like learning style models maintain the myth of unlimited resources is that they are developed and evaluated entirely on the basis of their scientific merit, i.e., their theoretical logic and research validity. This myth of sufficiently scientifically respectable theoretical model directly influencing practice not only ignores practitioner resources, but also fails to consider the implicit theories teachers have used in the past to guide their practice. (More about this later.) As with the other two myths, the effect is to cut teachers off from their own experience, and make its application less likely. (There is also considerable disagreement among experts in learning style and matching about whether theory/research have at this time provided a sufficient "database" from which to develop proposals, but this does not affect the myth since both groups of experts ignore teachers' implicit theories.)

## The Mystique of Learning Style

**Medical Model Mystique:** The 1979 NASSP monograph on learning style carries the subtitle "Diagnosing and Prescribing Programs"(Keefe, 1979) which clearly illustrates the medical model mystique. When you read that learning style application consists of "diagnosing" and "prescribing," how does it sound? Chances are you will feel that if you were to undertake such activity, you would need expert assistance at every step. To describe learning style applications in medical terms—"diagnosis," "prescribing"—also implies that something is wrong with the student which needs to be treated, further evidence of the need for expert assistance. In both cases, the idea of learning style becomes foreign to you as a teacher, and you are less able to tie it to your own experience.

**Test Mystique:** Each of the 30 or 40 learning style models provides its own specific test questionnaire for measuring those characteristics of learning style in the model. These are not achievement or ability tests, they are self-report tests; respondents are invited to express their preferences, self-judgments, and self-evaluations. Yet because they are published "tests," we are likely to endow them with some mystique, as if they were mental X-rays (the medical model again). Have you ever taken a short pop psychology test in a magazine which purported to measure your curiosity, sexiness, sense of humor, or whatever? What if your score disagreed with your own impression of yourself? If the thought entered your mind, "But this is a published test," then you know what "test mystique" is all about. I am not saying self-report measures are invalid or useless (indeed, I have concocted a few myself), only that they are simply systematic versions of your own self-judgment, not mental X-rays. It is not always easy to cut through such test mystique when considering learning style models because most are presented as "package deals" in which the test and model are inseparable [but they can be distinguished].

**Brain Mystique:** The claim that some learning styles are based on the psychology of the brain is at once persuasive and mystifying. For example, certain styles such as rational, systematic, linear ways of thinking are said to be controlled by the left side of the brain while creative, divergent, holistic ways of thinking are said to be controlled by the right side of the brain. The jargon of "right brain/left brain" has entered into our language to such an extent that it now occurs in the comic strip *Peanuts,* so you may wonder: Why call it mystical? First, note carefully that the evidence for right vs. left brain functioning is based entirely on studies of brain damaged persons and animals; it is highly unlikely that we will ever be able to measure brain activity directly to assess learning style. Second, the pattern of thinking described as "brain behavior"—systematic vs. intuitive, linear vs. holistic—has been present for thousands of years, and can legitimately be described in its own terms as different ways of experiencing. Third, such differences could equally well be described as Eastern thinking ("right brain") or Western thinking ("left brain"), since they correlate with these cultures. It's interesting to note how much more persuasive the claim seems in our culture if it's stated in terms of physiology rather than described by cultural correlates. Again, I am not taking issue with the research on brain behavior, only noting that when it is applied to the learning styles of non-brain damaged persons, it is nothing more than a metaphor (which could equally well be "Eastern vs. Western"), and we need to keep this in mind so that we are not mystified by the physiological reductionism. (Hunt, 1985, pp. 1–2)

# 4
# Teachers and Counselors Begin with Themselves

It may be that where there is a will there is a way but, no matter how willing, you are more likely to begin with yourself if you know the way. This chapter describes how to bring out your beliefs about your work, your concepts of your students, goals, and ways of teaching; your matching models; and your metaphor of teaching. Based on "How To Be Your Own Best Theorist" (Hunt, 1980a) in the Appendix, these self-instructional guides are appropriate for teachers and counselors as well as consultants, supervisors, theorists, researchers, and even nonprofessionals. Each group identifies concepts specific to its role—for example, when counselors go Inside-out to identify their theories, their concepts involve clients, aims, and counseling approaches, as contrasted with teachers' concepts about students, aims, and teaching approaches.

This chapter is written primarily for practitioners—teachers, counselors, therapists, social workers, and nurses. Chapter 5 is written especially for consultants, supervisors, and trainers, while Chapter 6 is directed to theorists and researchers. Whatever your professional stripe, I suggest that you read all three because they provide a broad sample of implicit theories and will enable you to better understand other professional roles, which should improve your communication and working relations. In a similar way, nonprofessional readers may become more aware of how professionals think about their work, and they may also be interested in trying out some of the exercises (like parents are theorists, too).

# Beginning with Practitioners

The reasons for reversing my motto to "There is nothing so theoretical as good practice" and for beginning to develop an Inside-out approach are much clearer to me now than they were during the 1970s. The seed for Inside-out was contained in my 1971 observation that "the task of implementing a matching model should begin with an investigation of what implicit matching model the educational decision maker is now using." Note that I first consider practitioners' implicit theories because the Outside-in approach to "implementing" my matching model was not always successful. Initially, I did not consider teachers' implicit theories to help them clarify their ideas; I did so to help implement my theory.

Later, as teachers brought out their theories in my learning styles graduate course, I saw how valuable they were to the teachers themselves. As I shared their implicit theories with others in the class, I realized that practitioners' experienced knowledge is the cornerstone of any theoretical account of practice—practice to theory. Now may be the right time for beginning with the practitioner, as illustrated in the following statement by Bird (1984) concerning the difficulties in implementation:

> More systematic attention to the obvious investments of persons in their present practices and arrangements would have advanced implementation. (p. 75)

This shift is also evident in the enormous increase in research on teacher thinking (e.g., Clark & Peterson, 1986). The recent popularity of teacher thinking seems to be a sign of accepting and respecting teachers' experienced knowledge, but caution is advised. Why are psychological theorists and educational researchers interested in teacher thinking? To develop conceptual models of teacher thinking (Outside-in)? To evaluate critically how teachers think (Outside-in)? To catalog the different kinds of thinking among different groups of teachers (Outside-in)? Or to help the teachers themselves clarify their thinking to form a foundation that enables them to communicate with other teachers and develop and extend their theories (Inside-out)?

Just as some psychologists study teacher thinking, others study consumer thinking to develop advertising campaigns geared to how consumers think and feel. Researchers in teacher thinking are not necessarily "hidden persuaders," but neither are they usually aiming to help teachers benefit from their research. The key question, therefore, is "Why do researchers study teacher thinking?" Teachers are keenly aware of the Outside-in purposes previously outlined and accordingly wary of researchers who want to study them. When I invite teachers to bring out their implicit theories, their initial reaction is that the purpose is for *my* research, not for their benefit. What else should they expect from a gray-bearded professor? How I try to counter this Outside-in interpretation is described in the next section.

# Why Should Practitioners Bring Out Their Theories?

Beginning with ourselves is not easy and before committing themselves, practitioners want answers to the following questions: What is the purpose? Who will decide whether and in what way my theories will be made public? Who will interpret them? Am I free to keep them to myself? Practitioners may not raise these questions openly, but they are nonetheless concerns. I have learned that unless the general answer is "For you to use in whatever way you choose" and unless I consistently reinforce this conviction through my actions, they are not likely to invest the energy, good will, and risk-taking required. An example of this approach can be seen in the way I work with practitioners to bring out their implicit theories in my learning styles course.

I have used Kelly's Rep Test to bring out the theories of hundreds of practitioners who have taken this class and, although I have collected several hundred of their implicit theories and matching models (with their permission), I have never used any of them for research purposes. Although they are available for all kinds of objective analysis, such as comparing concepts and theories of secondary vs. elementary or experienced vs. novice teachers, I have never used them for this "Outside-in" purpose. I did not consciously decide to refrain from analyzing these implicit theories: It was only in recent years, when my student colleagues sometimes asked whether teachers of adults use more motivational descriptions than teachers of young students, that I realized I had unconsciously avoided using them for my own purposes. I think I was trying to emphasize that all of these Inside-out activities were for one purpose only—for the teachers to use as they chose.

It is very difficult to describe how I try to create a climate of openness, trust, and good will. That I have not used their theories for my research is only one specific way. Others include how I address them (as colleagues), how I respond to their questions and comments (by accepting, by tying their remarks in with other comments, and by extending), and, perhaps most important, by conveying my belief that I can learn a great deal from them. What practitioners have brought out in this climate has affirmed my belief that they are theorists, too. (You can judge for yourself from the examples on the following pages.) I am also convinced that the samples of "teacher thinking" brought out in this trusting climate are much richer than those brought out when teachers are subjects in an experiment.

Although it is not easy, and some would say impossible, to create this climate on the printed page, I try to do so by invoking your good will and asking you to actually try the following miniature exercise.

# The Return of the Rep Test

In my first attempts to bring out practitioners' concepts in the early 1970s, I returned to using the Kelly Rep Test, which I had studied for my master's thesis. I invite you to try a miniature version of the Rep Test to obtain a first-hand experience of what it is like to bring out your implicit concepts. Why not indulge in my invitation to learn through experience? First you need six slips of paper or cards. Number each slip or card from 1 to 6, and write the name or initials of a person with whom you work on each card. If you are a teacher, use students; if a counselor, use clients; if an educational consultant, use teachers or other clients. If you are a theorist, try to become a practitioner and use your students or clients.

The basic Rep Test procedure is to consider the persons in groups of three, so begin by placing the three cards numbered 1, 2, and 3 in front of you. Next, answer the question "Which two of these three are most alike as students (or clients) in some important way?" Put those two persons together, separate from the third person. Then answer the final question—"How are they alike?"—and write down their similarities in a word or phrase on a separate sheet of paper titled "My Role Concept Repertory." Under this title make a list from 1 to 4. After #1 write your concept of their similarities, recording the numbers of the two cards you paired (e.g., 1 and 2—bodacious). You have just identified your first role concept. Identify three more, using the same procedure but looking at different groups of cards (second: 4, 5, 6; third: 1, 3, 5; and fourth: 2, 4, 6) so that you have a list of four descriptions, or role concepts. Try to use four *different* concepts.

In Kelly's terms this is your repertory of role concepts, a short list but a sample that shows how you might use your list for further understanding of your ideas. Do the concepts seem true for you? Are they really concepts that you use? What do they emphasize—achievement, motivation? How much do they tell you about how to approach these persons—If you knew only this much about them, would it help you to begin to work with them? I hope you are beginning to see the possibilities in learning more about your implicit concepts. Implicit theories are more than just our concepts of other persons; they also involve our goals and our approaches to trying to attain these goals, as described next.

# George Kelly, Meet Kurt Lewin!

As I mentioned earlier, teaching-learning transactions can be considered from Kurt Lewin's B = f (P, E) formula by translating it as learning outcome (Behavior) resulting from the interaction of student characteristics (Person) and teaching approach (Environment). The letters B, P, and E constitute a convenient shorthand to view the complexities of teaching and learning (Hunt & Sullivan, 1974). The Rep Test brought out your P(erson) concepts, but your concepts of B(ehavior) and E(nvironment) are needed as well. I therefore played a Lewinian variation on the Kelly theme, as follows.

Look at your response sheet and pull out the two persons you saw as alike. Look at them again and ask yourself "How are these two alike in terms of what I would like to see them learn?" Write this goal on your response sheet in a middle column labeled "Learning Outcomes (B)." Consider each of the other three groups of two persons in the same way, and fill in learning outcomes for them as well.

Before beginning the next step, label the left column "Student Characteristics (P)" and the right column "Teaching Approaches (E)." (Counselors should use "Client Characteristics" and "Counseling Approaches.") Then fill in the E column as follows. Again, remove the two persons originally compared and ask "How are these two alike in terms of how I might work with them?" and fill in your answer. Continue with the other three in the same way to identify your own teaching approach. If you have been participating, you now have 12 descriptions on your sheet that can serve as a foundation on which to bring out your theories of matching (that is, *if* this student characteristic, *then* this approach).

I realize that some of you may not have actually participated in this miniature exercise for one reason or another. Perhaps you don't like to interrupt your reading to do an exercise; perhaps you have a strong aversion to formulas and letter abbreviations and therefore tuned out, or perhaps you don't approve of classifying students as being alike or different because it seems to be "pigeonholing" or stereotyping.

Most of these feelings of resistance could have been overcome if you were actually participating in a workshop and not just reading about one, but another, more general kind of resistance is often experienced by many practitioners—one that might be described by the stinger "paralysis through analysis." Practitioners view their work as a total experience that must be considered as a whole.

When asked to break it into parts they frequently resist because they doubt the value of doing so (paralysis through analysis). For this reason I begin the complete series of *How To Be Your Own Best Theorist* exercises with an initial exercise to bring out the whole—how you see your work in its entirety—by writing a letter to an understanding colleague "about my work." This will give you an explicit "whole" foundation to serve as an anchor while you consider the parts. This approach should help overcome any fear of losing your work as it becomes only little bits and pieces. It should show how you will return to the whole once you have analyzed its parts and their relationships.

# How To Be Your Own Best Theorist II

The initial paper (Hunt, 1980a), containing instructions on how to bring out your beliefs, concepts, matching models, and metaphors, is summarized in the Appendix. One of my graduate student colleagues who brought out her theories in my learning styles class, Jane Gow, agreed to "go public" in "How To Be Your Own Best Theorist II" (Hunt & Gow, 1984). I appreciated both Jane's willingness to put her implicit theories into print and the journal's willingness to publish them. This publication shows that practitioners are theorists too, and I wish there were a journal, *Practitioner Theory and Research*. For now, I summarize the results of her becoming her own best theorist by providing the following excerpt.

### Exercise 1: About My Teaching

I strive to create a warm and inviting atmosphere in my classroom—one that will make my pupils feel both comfortable and enthusiastic about their learning environment. I want the children (and their parents) to feel that the time is being spent at worthwhile activities, both social and academic. I attempt to adapt these activities to suit the needs of the pupils, as difficult as this is at times.

Although maintaining a confident self-image is an important consideration, I also hope to challenge and stretch their capabilities.

Fostering independence is also a major goal. We spend a great deal of time and effort clarifying expectations and routines. A sense of order is important to me. I encourage self-directed learning, but I cannot function amid chaos; I feel control, either by the pupil himself or by the teacher, is necessary. Children can, and should, interact as they learn, but one child's behavior should not infringe on the rights or feelings of others.

We strive for excellence, but allowance must be made for those children who fall short of the mark. Standards have to be present, but are weighed carefully to allow for these individual differences.

As pupils leave my class each year, my main concern is not the content of what they have learned, but that they have an interest in learning and the tools to help them to learn how to learn. (Hunt & Gow, 1984, pp. 64–65)

## Exercise 2: About My Students (P Concepts)

Table 4–1 summarizes the lists of concepts which Jane Gow identified in Exercises 2, 3, and 4. Since the lists were produced and considered separately, for now consider only the list of person concepts on the left side.

**Reaction to My P Concepts:** As I attempted to sort the students, I found it difficult to come up with one word or a short phrase. I felt that I knew how the two students were alike, but the exact terminology eluded me. I was also concerned that in the cases where the characteristic was negative that it was a reflection on my teaching. I had taught them for an entire year and yet the characteristic still persisted.

**Accuracy of P Concepts:** I would say that these descriptions are definitely accurate for me. My goals are ones which relate to personal growth and I think this was reflected in these constructs. Perhaps the reason that these personal growth characteristics mean so much to me is that I was teaching grade one, and therefore felt my role was to equip my students with characteristics such as independence, responsibility, cooperation, etc., that they would need throughout the long school career that lay ahead of them.

**Comparison with Person Concepts of Colleagues:** A comparison of my P concepts with those of the others in the class indicated to me that my concepts certainly were not unique. I found each of my concepts at least once and in some cases up to six and seven times. This would have reassured me at the time that I was at least on the right track and that others would certainly be able to understand them because we used the same characteristics.

**Consideration of My P Concepts as Accessibility Characteristics:** I feel quite dissatisfied when I consider my P concepts in terms of accessibility characteristics. Few of my concepts tell me how to tune into the student. Concepts such as "poor reading skills" and "aggressive" tell me very little about the optimal environment for that student. "Hard-working" and "cooperative" convey a little more information about the child's motivational orientation, but even then I feel it is not clear enough. Terms such as "independent" and "lacks independence" come closer. In doing this again I would try to be more aware of these channels of accessibility and aim to consider them more carefully. (Hunt & Gow, 1984, pp. 65–67)

## Exercise 3: About My Outcomes (B Concepts)

**Reflections on B Concepts:** If the student characteristic was negative, it seemed rather obvious what I would list as my goal for that P concept. However, it was more difficult to state a learning outcome if the P concept was positive, e.g., independent. It seemed to go without saying that I would want to have the child maintain that characteristic. In this case I listed such B concepts as serving as a role model or leader.

**Accuracy of B Concepts:** Once again I feel these outcomes are the ones I emphasize in my teaching; they are accurate for me. These learning outcomes are goals that I feel are important for any and all pupils—even though this is very idealistic. My goals are not very specific, measurable, or observable.

**Comparison to B Concepts of Other Colleagues:** Others in the class seem to lean to the idealistic as well. The majority of goals seem to relate to social and emotional development, on a long-term basis, as I feel mine do. Very few learning outcomes are specific and short-term.

## Exercise 4: About My Approaches (E Concepts)

**Accuracy of My E Concepts:** The ten approaches are accurate for me. I may not have actually articulated some of them before, but I do most of these things intuitively.

**Comparison with E Concepts of Others in Class:** I noted that many members of the class described teaching approaches that were similar to my own. Suggestions such as more structure, praise and encouragement, small group activities, and role models appeared quite frequently in the other summary sheets. However, some members of the class were far more detailed and would provide another teacher with far more information for planning for the particular students.

## Table 4-1
## Summary Sheet of Person, Behavior, and Environment Concepts

| Student Characteristics—Person Concepts (Ex. 2) | Learning Outcomes—Behavior Concepts (Ex. 3) | Teaching Approaches—Environment Concepts (Ex. 4) |
|---|---|---|
| 1. socially isolated, intolerant of others | to interact more positively with peers | assign cooperative tasks and evaluate on group basis |
| 2. independent | to become a group leader | provide more responsibilities concerning choice of activity |
| 3. lack independence | to develop more independence | outline specific steps to accomplish each task |
| 4. cooperative | to serve as a role model | provide visibility, e.g. lead small groups |
| 5. aggressive | to control aggression | provide reward and encouragement for appropriate behavior |
| 6. poor reading skills | to become an independent reader | use own language as reading material |
| 7. imaginative | to strengthen and expand thinking process | assign tasks that require higher-level thinking skills |
| 8. shy | to build a more positive self-image | praise and encouragement of self-expression |
| 9. irresponsible | to develop self-control | outline specific expectations and time line |
| 10. hardworking | to feel work is satisfying and worthwhile | allow individual choice of activity and set own pace |

# Exercise 5: About My Matching Models (P-E Combinations)

These ten P-E combinations were then considered in terms of their underlying matching models. After reflecting on the process and comparing with others, participants were instructed to consider common criteria for judging matching models and to develop a metaphor for their matching model. (See *Bringing Out Your Matching Models* later in this chapter.)

The if-then pairing of the student characteristics and teaching approaches produced the following relationships which are grouped into four clusters.

- *maximizing* on a student's strength and extending the scope
- *reinforcement* of the positive dimension of a particular student behavior in order to reduce the negative dimension
- *imposing* more structure and segmenting each task into smaller, more specific chunks
- *compensating* for a deficit by providing more direct one-to-one teaching

**Reaction to My Matching Models:** Once I had established that there were similarities between some of my teaching approaches, it soon came about that all of my P concepts were dealt with in only four general categories. Establishing the matching relationship was extremely difficult at first. The reason could be that after a certain number of years in teaching, this match becomes almost automatic—which may be both good and bad! Then when one is required to stand back and describe this matching it becomes rather like stating the obvious. But, perhaps it is this stating of the obvious which is necessary in order to evaluate why we do what we do. Then, depending on your subjective evaluation, change and growth in one's teaching can occur.

**Comparison to Matching Models of Others in the Class:** I found that once again my results were similar to many other members of the class. Statements such as "if positive then more autonomy," "if negative then more structure" came through in several papers. In most cases, including my own, I would describe these relations as macro-matching or developmental rather than contemporaneous approaches.

**Criteria for Matching Statements:** Considering the realities and limitations of teaching on a daily basis, the one criterion that is obviously used most often by teachers is the personal criterion. It has been my experience that even teachers who have studied the theories and been presented with the empirical evidence rely heavily on their implicit theories. This intuitive approach has obvious limitations, i.e., incomplete or resistance to flexing, but even so is the basis of the teaching-learning interaction.

**My Matching Metaphor:** The matching metaphor that comes to my mind is the relationship between the gardener and his tomato plants. The children come to my class just like the small tomato plants, packaged and huddled together in a flimsy tomato box. I don't get the seeds—someone else started them off! I take them as established plants even though some are not well established; they may be damaged or in need of care, but at least they have started.

The first step is to separate them, gently, from their plastic packages and introduce them, carefully, to the new garden. Each tiny plant is set in the ground where it seems to fit most comfortably. The garden environment includes all the elements necessary for growth—water, food, light, and space.

With nurturing and time the plants begin to grow. Some grow quickly and without any special care. Others lean over or have damaged areas that need extra trimming or fertilizer. The strong, healthy ones continue to grow without much help from the gardener, and produce tiny white flowers as a sign that someday they will bear fruit. Some plants find it difficult to stand alone and therefore need a stake to lean on. Once this support has been given they are off and growing again. Other plants find their own support system, for example, the garden fence, and so can grow more independently.

Soon harvest time comes. Each plant is at a different stage of growth. Some have the tiny white flowers, others have the hard, green tomatoes, and others have the beautiful red tomatoes ready for picking. But each plant has something to show for its growth. (Hunt & Gow, 1984, p. 67)

## Identifying My Learning Style

[This exercise was added to the original exercises and is quite similar to "Identifying Your Own Learning Style" in Chapter 3.]

I feel I learn best when the task or material is laid out for me in a systematic, step-by-step way. The procedure or concepts come easiest to me when they are broken down into small steps. The optimal approach for me seems to be visual and hands-on when possible. If this is not possible, then various parallel examples or analogies would help. Questioning the presenter and being able to find out the reason "why" is also important to me, and therefore helps my learning.

Consequently, I use this same systematic style in my teaching, especially when the topic or concept is new or when a student appears to be having difficulty. Once the situation is more familiar to the children or they have indicated a certain competence, then I am more likely to open up the structure and allow for more lateral moves rather than strictly vertical.

This exercise has certainly heightened my awareness about my learning style. I am now aware of how much I might be imposing my style on others. It is a rather uncomfortable feeling at present, and one with which I will have to "flex" to at a conscious level. (Hunt & Gow, 1984, p. 68)

## Final Exercise: Restatement "About My Teaching"

As I re-examine my original statement, I feel that I can still support most of what I said there. I am concerned more with personal growth than cognitive goals and the preceding exercises verify that for me.

One concern I have now is the lack of attention I paid to accessibility characteristics. If I were to add to my original statement, I would attempt to address this, and consequently be more specific.

I am well aware now of how I impose, not only my learning style, but also my value system upon my students. I'm certain that this is unavoidable to a certain extent, but now especially as I work with adults rather than first graders, this must become one of my major goals. [Note: She is now a primary grade consultant.] (Hunt & Gow, 1984, p. 68)

## Dialogue Between Authors About Exercises

*DH:* Jane, I was especially interested in your matching ideas. You did all of these exercises before reading any theory or research on matching, yet your matching ideas—for example, maximizing, compensating—are very similar to those the researchers have identified. Could you comment on how you came to those ideas in your matching theories?

*JG:* At first it was very difficult. I'd never taken the time to state these things out loud. I remember working at it very hard, just thinking. I suppose in teacher training I came across these expressions but they hadn't been used as such ... other than perhaps in writing report cards. So it was searching back to find the word that captures this matching relationship.

*DH:* Did that happen quickly?

*JG:* No, it was a struggle. I struggled and struggled, and all of a sudden I looked over all at once, and then the light came on. I thought "If this happens then this is what I do" ... and I do it more or less intuitively and I don't put it into words. So if I see a child in this particular situation I know ... maybe from experience, maybe from teacher training ... that that's what I'll do ... and I never had said that before.

*DH:* How did you feel about your matching notions once they were on paper?

*JG:* Some of them seemed very obvious. Of course if a child can't do something or lacks something then I feel my role is to be sure, to take him through a process where he'll be able to do that. So it seems overstating the obvious. Where the characteristic was positive, I thought, well the only thing to do with the positive characters is to hope it continues . . . try to reinforce it and make sure it stabilizes.

*DH:* Sometimes I think teachers have the feeling when they push to this level of abstraction that it's no longer useful. They may feel that in the classroom you have to match to the individual student. How do you feel about that?

*JG:* I thought it would be useful because it's not totally individualized . . . I have to go back and think, have I ever taught a child like this before? What did I do then that worked? Could it apply to this child? If not, although we say that children are unique, they're not totally unique. Some of them have the same characteristics . . . so if I had experienced this before—if this happened, then what did I do—I would apply the same matching here.

*DH:* Now that you're working as a consultant, do you find any of these ideas are useful in your communication with teachers?

*JG:* Yes [pause], I don't know that it's as useful when it's someone else. They have to come to the realization that I came to myself—so although I want to tell them, it doesn't always help.

*DH:* [laughing] Touché!

*JG:* It doesn't always help just for me to say I have experienced children like this before and this is what I did. Some teachers will take it and use it well. Others, because they don't deeply believe in it, they misuse it and it doesn't work for them; then they say it was my fault since they didn't really experience it.

*DH:* I wonder if there's any way we could shorten the time required to identify these ideas. In your consulting would there be any way to help the teachers get in touch with some of their own matching ideas more quickly?

*JG:* The metaphor process . . . on a very simple level. Just ask them what they think. . . . I think it would help me as a consultant to know what their own theory of learning is, their own theory of teaching, so I know how to help them. If they see teaching as a medical metaphor, if they visualize it as a gardening metaphor, that helps me to get in touch with them.

*DH:* Could you comment on how your seeing the summary sheets and matching ideas of others in our class affected your own identifying of your theory?

*JG:* I think because the experience was so different and so unique I really felt I didn't know where I was going. I wanted that feedback that I'm on the right track . . . but it wasn't until I heard their comments in class and maybe out of class . . . that some of them were having difficulty with it as well . . . or some of them didn't know what to do with it . . . then when I saw on paper that they were coming out with the same kind of . . . especially when I compared my outcomes with their outcomes and saw so many similarities that it reassured me that I was on the right track . . . and it was something maybe I should go through. First of all, to be asked to make explicit what we don't always get asked to do, to state it out blank, point blank. . . .

*DH:* You've never been asked that before?

*JG:* No, I never had. I suppose I did it personally when I had to write a report card for a child but I never really had to state the theory as such . . . conversations of teachers don't get to theory . . . they get to personalities, they get to strategy . . . I find in my role as consultant, teachers want the practice, the strategies . . . not necessarily the theory. It's the rare teacher that wants this.

*DH:* But doesn't the strategy have to be in some kind of implicit theory? Otherwise it's just a bag of tricks?

*JG:* Mmhuh, but that's my fear, that it is just a bag of tricks that we consultants deliver. . . . The teachers believe that the consultant has the time to be the theorist and then comes up with a bag of tricks . . . but if you don't know the theory as well, when you go to put it into practice and it's not working out well, you don't have the resources to go back and see what went wrong because you're using somebody else's tricks.

*DH:* Could you say something about how identifying your own learning style and teaching style fit in?

*JG:* That was something I'd never done on such a conscious level either . . . I experienced it in my new role as consultant because I was working with someone who had done it perhaps on the intuitive level and was aware of her own learning style. We were finding that we were at different ends and at the time that I had to do these exercises it coincided beautifully in that I did learn something . . . perhaps even intuitively . . . about my own learning style.

*DH:* I really have been delighted with the experience you've had because I think it illustrates what I hoped would happen. I hoped that there was a sense of affirmation of what you and your colleagues, as teachers, know.

*JG:* Well, I've always been told right from the beginning of my teaching career that you should have your own philosophy of education, your own theory of education . . . but always thinking that I don't have time to stop and do it. So now I realize that I do have a theory and I have taken the time to do it.

*DH:* Great! (Hunt & Gow, 1984, pp. 68–69)

Jane Gow's concepts in Table 4–1 and her matching models show the benefits that are possible from becoming your own best theorist. Doing so provides the opportunity for you, like any theorist, to put your theory to the test. For example, in the first P-E combination in Table 4–1 (if a student is socially isolated, then assign cooperative tasks and evaluate on a group basis), Jane may choose to "experiment" on this matching idea to find out if it works just as formal theorists attempt to verify their theories through experiments.

Bringing out your own theory is a first step, and what happens next is up to you. You may look at your own concepts and matching ideas and decide you like them just as they are. Or you may want to change your ideas and use your present implicit theory as a blueprint for change. How you use it is entirely up to you, and this is one of the most important messages to convey.

Before presenting other examples of theories brought out by practitioners, I should mention that I have revised and extended the "How To Be Your Own Best Theorist" exercises considerably since the paper was published in 1980 (Hunt, 1980a in Appendix 1). These revisions include: (1) identifying your own metaphor through guided imagery; (2) beginning the exercises with identifying your own learning style for the reasons shown in Chart 1 in Chapter 3; (3) emphasizing that the letter about your work, matching model, and metaphor are all related to one another in revealing your implicit theory; and (4) developing a method—the CREATE cycle described in Chapter 8—to apply your implicit theories as well as to help you communicate your experienced knowledge.

I have emphasized that the major purpose of practitioners' bringing out their theories should be for their own use. How does my including samples of their theories in my book fit in with this belief? First, I do not maintain that practitioners should not participate in research about their implicit theories; they may choose to do so on their own or in a collaborative venture, as Jane Gow did with me.

As for the graduate student colleagues in my learning style classes over the past ten years, I have given them the choice of allowing their papers to be copied anonymously so that future students could see how practitioners can become their own best theorists, and most of them have agreed. I have also asked the three classes I taught since beginning work on this book if they were willing to have portions of their theories appear and, since my purpose is to affirm experienced knowledge and empower practitioners, most of them have also enthusiastically agreed. In the case of Mary Shawcross, whose implicit theories are presented in the following section, and the two colleagues whose theories appear in Chapter 5, they have agreed to join Jane Gow in going public. In other cases excerpts are used anonymously.

# A Counselor Brings Out Her Theories

Mary Shawcross is a public health nurse who works as a counselor/teacher in the community. She brought out her implicit theories in my class and has agreed to have them presented here.

**About My Work (summarized):**
- to be "in touch" with the learner with whom I am communicating
- to create a stimulating atmosphere of learner participation
- to summarize my teaching at the end of a session so that there can be a review of the experience and an opportunity for the learner to indicate how the learning experience has been for him/her and how learning can be applied in his/her own situation

**Concepts About Clients, Goals, and Counseling Approaches:** Concepts about clients, goals, and counseling approaches appear in Table 4–2.

**My Matching Model:** In examination of my P-E relations, I have been able to group them mainly into four teaching approaches. While I believe these four areas demonstrate aspects of my teaching style, they are based also on my learning style. I *focus* on developing the individual's basic feelings of self-worth and stimulate him/her to be involved in activity to promote self-development. When I feel an individual is too self-centered, I *encourage* him/her to extend him/herself to learn to relate to others, to reduce over-self-focusing and to increase development of peer relationships. For an individual who is secure within him/herself and can participate in group activities, I *discuss* being receptive to new ideas and new activities so that the individual's development does not remain static or deteriorate. For the very few people I encounter who are striving to extend themselves beyond their present state of learning, I try to *maximize* their endeavors through encouragement and praise.

Generally, the more secure an individual is of him/herself and can expand beyond self, the less directive and imposing I am in my teaching style.

**Metaphors:** My metaphor of counseling: I picture myself as the magician who keeps all the plates spinning on the long rods and has to keep running back and forth to keep the plates going and prevent them from falling and breaking.

My metaphor of matching: I am a chameleon-like guide on the road of life approaching others in their life voyage. For many, I am an advocate, a nurturer, and a director; for others, I am a reflector for their experiences; and, for a few, I am a stimulator-supporter.

If there is value in practitioners' sharing concepts and matching models, there seems to be even greater value in their sharing and comparing their metaphors. I return to this in describing the CREATE cycle in Chapter 8, where Mary's magician metaphor appears again.

## Table 4–2
## Summary Chart of a Counselor

| | Client Characteristics (P) | Learning Outcomes (B) | Counseling Approaches (E) |
|---|---|---|---|
| 1. (1) (4) 8 | short attention span; self-centered | to interact with peers in small groups or dyads | introduce individual to peer for mutual support |
| 2. (2) 5 (9) | weak self concept | to develop feelings of self-worth | stimulate efforts of individual in setting own course of action |
| 3. (3) (7) 10 | inquisitive | to increase exploratory abilities | outline an activity promoting multiple alternatives |
| 4. (4) (6) 11 | fearful of new environments | to become involved with a peer support group | accompany individual to a peer support group, for the first time |
| 5. (1) (5) 12 | domineering; want to feel in control of situations | to initiate a self-directed learning experience | allow individual to problem solve with little direction |
| 6. (2) 6 (9) | easily distracted; irresponsible | to become responsible and dependable | contract with individual, completion of a task |
| 7. (3) (4) 10 | self-centered; inflexible | to develop some outside interests | encourage individual to select activity, involving another person |
| 8. (5) 6 (11) | cynical, especially of something new | to be receptive to something new | discuss with individual feelings, trying something new |
| 9. (7) (8) 9 | hardworking, dependable | to feel efforts are satisfying and worthwhile | commend efforts of individual in working through something difficult |
| 10. (10) 11 (12) | isolated, few outside interests | to interact with peers in group environment | foster individual's sharing of a skill with others |

# Bringing Out Your Matching Models

Although we are matching throughout our lives, identifying our matching models—considering *why* we choose one matched approach rather than another—is by no means simple. In the example of matching in the moment outlined in Chapter 3, the reason for choosing to draw a map (E) to direct (B) a stranger (P) is straightforward; the stranger did not understand English well, and therefore a nonverbal approach seemed appropriate. However, when "reading" your student or client, there are many approaches from which to choose, such as the two different approaches in Tables 4–1 and 4–2 to the same characteristic, "isolated."

The first step in bringing out your matching model (P-E relations) is to copy the Person characteristic and Environmental approach from your response sheet on the miniature Rep Test. (If you did not bring out your own concepts, use those of Jane Gow in Table 4–1.) The form is as follows:

> *If* [Person characteristic], *then* [Approach] because . . .
>
> In Jane Gow's case, the first two are:
> 1. If the student is isolated, then I assign cooperative tasks and evaluate on a group basis because _____.
> 2. If the student is independent, then I provide more responsibilities concerning choice of activity because _____.
>
> [Note that in the bottom row of Table 4–2, Mary Shawcross also used the description "isolated" but a slightly different approach "foster individual's sharing of skill with others" which might have a differnt basis in matching.]

Working out the reason for your particular choice is a very demanding cognitive task requiring you to form a *relational* concept between two of your concepts, but most practitioners find it is worth the effort, e.g., "This exercise forced me to write down my thoughts and really 'think' about *why* I would do something in a class even though intuitively I would know it was the best thing to do and just do it." I provide a worksheet for participants to record ten P-E combinations and then try to bring out the reason for their choice. Sometimes there may be little or no relationship between a particular P-E pair, but participants usually identify several P-E relationships from the ten P-E pairs on which to build their matching concepts.

Practitioners often question the practical value of describing their work in highly abstract language, language that seems remote from the realities of their practice (i.e., they do not want to become their own theorists if it means a complete retreat to the ivory tower of general abstractions). I point out that self-knowledge, whether concrete or abstract, may be valuable and use Jane Gow's

## Teachers and Counselors 71

matching models as an example. Identifying the four processes—maximizing strength, reinforcing to reduce negative features, imposing more structure, and compensating for a deficit—raised her awareness about the purposes of her matching and allowed her to choose from them. Although abstract, these matching models can be brought to bear in a concrete way in working with specific students or clients.

Participants may say why they choose a specific P-E combination by restating the purpose (B): The reason for the first P-E combination is "to interact more positively with peers." It is quite true in B-P-E terms that the aim of the particular P-E combination is to produce the desired B, but participants are encouraged to probe more deeply into *how* this E will lead to the desired outcome.

Although I was an Outside-in expert on matching models, I have learned much more about their practical value during the last few years by helping practitioners work Inside-out. In recent class discussions, considering the variety with which the 25 participants expressed their matching models, we realized that they can be expressed as (1) *action,* (2) *process,* and (3) *basic belief.* Using the counselor's matching models, for example, the specific "If P, then E" relations illustrate the action level; e.g., "I introduce the individual to peers for mutual support." Matching-as-process is shown by "focusing, encouraging, discussing, and maximizing" while basic beliefs are not explicitly expressed but might include such general ideas as "balance," "unity," "symmetry," and so on.

Because this task is so demanding and sometimes ambiguous, participants welcome the opportunity to show their matching models (identified only by code letters). They are relieved to discover that many of their colleagues also had difficulty and not everyone produced a tight, logical model; they are affirmed when they see that others have brought out ideas similar to their own; and they are stimulated by new possibilities that they may not have considered.

The following excerpts, taken from some of the participants' matching models, show the variety in the models and how sharing this variety enhances practitioners' understanding. Probably the most frequent model is to maximize strength and compensate for weakness, as shown below.

> I find that it is difficult to establish the matching relationship between my P and E concepts since I seldom come to evaluate or think about it even though I have been teaching for a few years. This matching model helps me to realize that I am not only concerned with the transmission of knowledge but also with the personal growth of the students. It is really important for us to think of what and why we use that approach when dealing with different types of students. From my own matching model, I realize that for those students that have negative characteristics, my approach will usually emphasize their positive development and at the same time control their negative attitude. For those that are bright and positive, I tend to give them a

chance to widen and strengthen their talents. When reflecting on my own teaching objectives, I find that I am quite consistent with this matching, but, practically, some are successful and others are not due to limitations and environmental factors. Anyway, this matching model serves as a guideline for my teaching approaches.

Following is a counselor's variation on the strength and weakness theme:

> The overall goal is to help the client become aware of his/her strengths and weaknesses and to work to enhance the former and to accept or change the latter. The three categories are interrelated of course, but as I look at the ten pairings I see that one usually takes precedence. I first determine the stage that the client is at. Then if he/she is confused or unaware, I focus on developing awareness of self, others, and/or the reality of a situation.
>
> If he/she presents me with a concern and seems to know what is happening but has attitudes or thoughts that are leading to inappropriate behavior or negative feelings/moods, I focus on the inappropriate cognitions.
>
> If he/she expresses a desire to change in a particular way/direction and if there seems to be an awareness of what that implies along with the appropriate cognitions, I use a more behavioral approach. I find it difficult to separate characteristics from the presenting problem or desired outcome; consequently, my matching model reflects both. It is also merely a framework since nothing is so clear-cut that it would fall directly into one of the categories.

Following are two examples at the "action" level:

1. If students are loners yet persevere, then "one-on-one" tasks lead to personalized attention, therefore success!
2. Bright yet skeptical students achieve at higher levels if allowed to work independently and inductively.
3. Quiet students should be encouraged to work cooperatively in groups to share ideas and information.
4. Small, short tasks lead to immediate feedback for students unsure of themselves.

\* \* \*

1. If a student is shy and withdrawn then I provide small group activities because these ease the sharing of ideas and build a support system.
2. If a student is confident and outgoing then I provide opportunities for small group leadership because students learn from role models.
3. If a student is dependent I focus on teaching problem-solving skills because this helps to build independence.
4. If a student has difficulty speaking I provide opportunities for presentations because this builds communication skills and confidence.

Following are two examples at the "process" level:

*Expanding* an individual's awareness, capability and responsibility, for those with demonstrated ability.
*Reducing and focusing* the tasks of those with limited ability.
*Involving* those at all levels in assigned tasks, on a continuum related to their individual capability.
*Instructing* those with knowledge deficits.
*Allowing autonomy* to high achievers who require stimulation.
*Minimizing* the peer influence of motivated achievers.

\* \* \*

- Emphasize that students recognize and use their peers as valuable learning resources.
- Design components in such a way that will build up the learner's level of (1) confidence and (2) independent action and learning.
- Encourage the use of observing, thinking, reflecting time to add more to a learning situation.
- Focus on the importance of the "person" in the whole learning situation.

After sharing matching models, participants frequently express a desire to revise and extend their own and are encouraged to do so. One of the benefits of bringing out their matching models is that they can be revised and extended, just as formal theories of matching. The response of the participants to sharing their B-P-E sheets, their matching models, and their metaphors as well as to reading Jane Gow's theory illustrates a dilemma in balancing Inside-out with Outside-in. I first became aware of this tension in my class several years ago when I did not make the Outside-in readings available until they had completed their Inside-out work. Some student colleagues were delighted with the opportunity to begin with themselves, unfettered by formal theories and research; others, however, were very unsettled (some even looked in the library for the Outside-in references that I held back). I now always discuss this issue, pointing out that it is up to them whether to read formal theories, earlier class papers, or Jane Gow's theory before bringing out their own theories, and their choice is probably an important indicator of their own style. Indeed, the availability of this book will complicate this issue even more.

Just as the participants' reactions to going Inside-out vary, so do their responses to the different approaches to identifying their implicit theories: their letters about their beliefs and intentions, their matching models, and their metaphors. I encourage them to look intensively for similarities in the three approaches, which will indicate basic features of their implicit theories, and to consider which approaches work best for them. The following excerpt shows how this practitioner found that the matching model approach worked better than the letter:

> I do not really see a great relationship between my letter and my matching models. I feel that they are of two different modes/domains. The letter appears to be descriptive more of the program and not necessarily of my teaching per se. I suppose I started at the wrong end—especially with a time limit of five minutes. My matching models seem to be more in the affective domain as opposed to being totally skill and behaviorally oriented.
>
> I feel that my matching models are much more reflective of my metaphor. They cover a wide range of activities and are concerned with the different areas pertinent to the development of the whole child: physical, cognitive, social, emotional, spiritual, and aesthetic.

Even though practitioners do not aspire to become Ivory Tower theorists, they are usually interested to note, in reviewing their own matching models and those of their classmates, that they have "rediscovered" the matching processes found by theorists of matching and ATI in their theories and research [e.g., the compensatory and preferential models (Snow, 1970) and the inducement and remedial model (Salomon, 1971)]. That practitioners have brought out these models (and others) in every class I have taught affirms my belief in the primacy of practice and in the necessity of beginning with practitioners' experienced knowledge. It is also true that when practitioners bring out student-client characteristics, they identify most of the important individual differences and learning styles already identified by formal theories and research.

I conclude this section with two excerpts from participants' exercises showing an awareness that could lead to change.

> With respect to my reading and flexing (P-E), I note that I tend to be more forceful and confrontative with people who do not meet my expectations but seem open to change. It appears that I am learning to respect people who feel a need for structure and control and am able to provide more direction and prescription than normal.
>
> \* \* \*
>
> These exercises have helped me to state student characteristics, learning outcomes, and teaching approaches more concisely and precisely. I noticed too that I tend to focus more on student weaknesses and attempt to strengthen them.

# Bringing Out Your Metaphors

Experienced practitioners are at a distinct disadvantage because they do not have an agreed-upon language to communicate with each other about their work. Because teachers and counselors do not have a vocabulary rooted in their experienced knowledge of their craft, they are forced to adopt the language of the theorist and researcher (i.e., from Outside). This lack of language is especially evident when experienced practitioners try to describe their specific actions, as in how they teach or how they counsel. I have therefore recently been exploring the possibility that practitioners' metaphors and images of their work may provide an alternative language for their communication. I encourage participants to generate personal metaphors and give some examples of them in the following pages.

I start by using some metaphors on my own in discussing certain features of the matching process in the following excerpt from "How To Be Your Own Best Theorist II" (Hunt & Gow, 1984).

## Formal or Intuitive Matching?

> Rather than rely on teachers' intuitive knowledge, most formal matching models use logical derivation and research evidence to support their claims for matching statements. Formal matching models need more than tight logic and weighty evidence to influence classroom practice directly; they must be compatible with teachers' intuitive matching. Since teachers must translate formal matching into their practice, these formal ideas should be expressed as metaphors compatible to those of teachers. Formal matching models are often presented as means for diagnosis and prescription, and here Kusler's comments (1982) are to the point:
>
>> "Diagnosing and prescribing" is a metaphor perhaps as harmful as it is useful. Its utility lies in the fact that it asks us to see each learner and his or her condition separately; its disservice is that it can suggest that learners are sick and that teachers are healers. In fact, if teachers really begin to see themselves as healers or rescuers, they'll require an ever-fresh supply of flawed beings needing their service!
>>
>> A substitute for the medical metaphor would describe teachers as discoverers and nurturers. Rather than "diagnose" a problem and its causes, the teacher would use all possible methods to discover the combinations of qualities that best define a person as a learner. The teacher no longer cries, "I see

what your problem is," but rather, "how much you can do!"
And in the process, the teacher helps the student to better know
himself or herself, especially as a whole and healthy being.
(Kusler, 1982, p. 11)

## Immediate or Developmental Matching?

Learning style may be considered an accessibility channel to which we tune (immediate matching) or it may itself be the object of change and enhancement (developmental matching). In working with a student whose most accessible channel is visual, do we provide only visual material (immediate) or intentionally use approaches through other modalities (developmental)? George Stern's frequently quoted metaphors of contented cows and aggravated oysters exemplify, among other things, an emphasis on immediate and developmental matching, respectively. (Stern, 1961)

## Preferred or Required Matching?

Is student learning style identified by the student's own preference or by someone else's judgment about what the student needs? Students are often asked to express preference without adequate experience of the learning options. If student preference is considered in terms of a cafeteria or library browsing metaphor, then appropriate emphasis is given to providing concrete experiences on which students can base their preferences. When someone else decides by use of a test or observation, then the metaphor is that of personnel selection where an "expert" classifies the applicant before placement.

## Teacher Style or Teaching Approach?

Students may be matched to a teacher's preferred style which may be limited, or to a particular teaching approach which may require the teacher to go beyond the preferred style. In the former, the metaphor is that of computer dating where the idea is to match students and teachers in a point-to-point fashion to minimize personality clashes and maximize interpersonal harmony. In the latter, the teacher is more like a utility infielder who has the versatility to play different roles and to provide a variety of approaches.

## One-Way or Two-Way Matching?

We usually think of matching in terms of the unilateral effect of teachers on students, yet students also exert an important influence on teachers in a two-way transaction. Unilateral matching is like a medical prescription dispensed to a patient without regard to the influence of the patient on the diagnosis or how the prescription will work when the patient changes. This is the UFO model: *U*nilateral, *F*ixed, and *O*bjective. By contrast, reciprocal matching acknowledges the give-and-take between student and teacher in a metaphor of orchestrating two instruments playing together or spontaneously improving variations on a theme, as when jazz musicians "trade fours." (Hunt & Gow, 1984, p. 70)

The most valuable approach I have found to help practitioners bring out their metaphors is through guided imagery exercises in which I ask them to imagine their work setting—classroom or office—and then allow an image or symbol to emerge. For many practitioners, this kind of guided imagery helps them identify their own metaphors, images, or symbols even though they may never have been aware of them before.

Guided imagery helps practitioners find their own personal metaphor from Inside-out rather than selecting one from Outside. Some student colleagues describe the process of searching for the most appropriate metaphor as difficult (e.g., "It took me quite a while to find my metaphor") while others do so very quickly. In either case, the metaphors are collected and distributed to the group.

Table 4-3 provides a list of metaphors initially brought out in my most recent class after the first guided imagery exercise. As with other exercises, the experience is amplified when participants share their metaphors, as shown here.

### Table 4-3
### Metaphors in October 1985 Learning Styles Class

- My work is like the wind blowing leaves in different directions.
- My work is like Christ's role as a teacher, especially by example.
- My work is like . . . a river fed by springs.
- My work is like an orchestra conductor (sometimes like a social worker).
- My work is like that of a *guide*—guiding over the rocky trail, giving support, helping people reach their goals.
- My work is like a band leader.
- My teaching is like life.
- My class is like a family.

- I'm a conductor on a train (the learning) and passengers (clients) get on and off when they decide. They choose their own destinations.
- I picture myself as the magician who keeps all the plates spinning on the long rods and has to keep running back and forth to keep the plates going and preventing them from falling and breaking.
- My work is like a sunflower.
- My work is like an open door/fruitful tree.
- My work is like a tourist guide bringing along a group of tourists to tour around a certain place, explaining to them in detail the famous things.
- My work is like "Climb a Mountain" counseling.
- My work is like going up a down escalator.
- My work is like guiding mountain-climbers/explorers.
- My work is like concealed beauty in a paradise.
- My work is like . . . a free-flowing handful of sand.
- My counseling is like being a fellow pilgrim—a fellow traveler along the path of life.
- My counseling is like being a loving mirror. My clients can see themselves though my eyes—and not experience judgment.
- My work is like being a "mother hen" gathering her chicks around her.

I am so enthusiastic about metaphors and images providing practitioners with a language for sharing their work that I must remind myself to respect each colleague's privacy and to allow him to make his own choice about "going public." When the participants in my class have come to know and trust one another, however, they are usually very willing to share their own and consider other metaphors. Of major value to practitioners is taking the metaphor literally and seeing what it provides (e.g., thinking of teaching as being like a harbor master could lead to considering just how a harbor master would organize his "class"). Chapter 8 describes how practitioners bring their metaphors to bear on their practical concerns and share them to develop new action plans.

Practitioners have generated hundreds of metaphors in my classes, and here I select three—all involving water—to show the richness of variation on this one topic. (Each of these three participants was in a different class in a different year.)

## Metaphor: The Ocean

The ocean's rhythms have always felt strong, secure and constant to me. My experience with dance leads me to kinesthetic metaphors and the ocean metaphor does not refer to the ocean's sound, color, smell or taste, but rather to its movement. I feel this movement—small and sometimes apparently unconnected or chaotic on the surface but constant and unified underneath in the relationship with the significant other in my life and with both my roles in the teaching/learning process.

The rhythm of the ocean represents the way things are and want to be. The rhythm in teaching and learning often feels congested or chaotic on the surface but underneath, the movement is always toward growth and toward an environment where this can occur. The ocean moves toward me, sprays and roars and pulls back, but always moves toward me again. My students and I move toward each other, interact, and move back but always somehow move toward each other again. The rhythm I feel in teaching—the calm, the storms, the ebbs and flows—still seems right to me.

There is always a risk near the ocean, especially the North Atlantic. There is a danger line across which one takes great risk to travel. Similarly, in teaching, there is a safety zone behind content and routine but the real learning and teaching seem to take place at the point of highest and yet, therefore, lowest risk.

There is intense energy and calm all at once in an ocean. There is intense energy and calm all at once in teaching.

## Metaphor: Gurgling, Rushing Stream

When I first reflected upon this metaphor as it came during the guided imagery, the essential descriptors were: life giving, active, pervasive, peaceful, harmonious, not fearful. Some of the important statements were:

- passing this way but once, make the best possible use of this time and these opportunities;
- want to leave others happy, invigorated, knowing their own worth and aware of their own inner and outer resources;
- influencing and being influenced (two-way opening and sharing process).

Later reflection revealed the apparent contradiction of adjectives, i.e., gurgling and gushing. Two very different activities are represented in these words. Only as I have relived the course's content and process for the purposes of this paper, can I see the extremes within myself, within my students and within my work environment. My metaphor seems to be depicting the diversity within myself to adapt itself to those students who need (gurgling) a more even, enthusiastic, co-responsible, cheerful, and supportive environment. This is definitely more in keeping with my usual human interactions and teaching approach. However, I am capable of strength (gushing), seeming strictness, and maintaining control. Considering what I have written before, I might be asking myself "So why worry about the apparent contradictions?" Quite simply, the gurgling aspect of the stream is my preferential style; it is also less demanding and less draining for me. Perhaps with time, more experience, increased confidence, and quiet reflection I will be able to integrate these two life forces into one. The metaphor conveys that vision, that hope.

### Metaphor: The Waterfall

Life is the waterfall as it proceeds from start to finish. The water is the individual learners as they try out different routes and seek to grow in awareness of themselves and truth. The spirit of the rocks is the teacher, taking various shapes and forms, sometimes creating tremendous visible impact and sometimes a more subtle effect. The spirit of the rock accepts all the water that comes its way and attempts to make it the most beautiful that it can be in its own way—sometimes spectacular and sometimes simple and ponderous but always contributing to the flow of life. This has become my metaphor for teaching.

## Personal Theories of Teaching

Fox (1983) used a different method—asking teachers "What do you mean by teaching?"—to bring out their implicit theories, which he then classified into four types: (1) transfer theories, (2) shaping theories, (3) traveling theories, and (4) growth theories. He elaborates on these in Table 4–4.

Fox's work is a good example of how to bring out teachers' implicit theories and organize them to be used Outside-in.

## Table 4-4
## Personal Theories of Teaching

| SUMMARY SHEET | Transfer Theory | Shaping Theory | Traveling Theory | Growing Theory |
|---|---|---|---|---|
| Verbs commonly used | Convey, impart, implant, imbue, give, expound, transmit, put over, propound, tell. | Develop, mold, demonstrate, produce, instruct, condition, prepare, direct (give orders). | Lead, point the way, guide, initiate, help, show, direct (show the way). | Cultivate, encourage, nurture, develop, foster, enable, help, bring out. |
| The subject matter | Commodity to be transferred, to fill a container. | Shaping tools, pattern, blueprint. | Terrain to be explored. Vantage points. | Experiences to be incorporated into developing personality. |
| The student | Container to be filled. | Inert material (clay, wood, metal) to be shaped | Explorer. | Developing personality, growing plants. |
| The teacher | Pump attendant, food processor, barmaid. | Skilled craftsman working on raw material or selecting and assembling components. | Experienced and expert travelling companion. Guide. Provider of travelling aids. | Resource provider. Gardener. |
| Standard teaching methods | Lectures, reading lists, duplicated notes. | Laboratory, workshop, practical instructions like recipes. Exercises with predictable outcomes. | Simulations, projects, etc. Exercises with unpredictable outcomes. Discussions, independent learning. | Experiential methods similar to travelling theory but less structured and more spontaneous. |
| Monitoring progress | Measuring and sampling contents of vessel. | Checking size and shape of product. | Comparing notes with travelling companion. | Listening to reflections on personal development. |
| Explanations of failure—teachers view | Leaky vessels, small container. | Flawed, faulty raw material. | Blinkered vision, lack of stamina. Unadventurous, lethargic. | Poor start, inadequately prepared, no will to develop. |
| Explanations of failure—students view | Poor transfer skills, poor aim. | Incompetent craftsman. Poor or missing blueprint. | Poor guides, poor equipment, too many restrictions on route. | Restricted diet, unsuitable food. Incompetent gardener. |
| Attitude to training | Need simple skills of transfer. | Need shaping to British Standard Teacher. | Need skills of expert guide as well as knowledge of terrain. | Need skills of diagnosing needs of individual plants. |

*Source:* Fox, 1983, p. 163

# Practitioners' Experiencing and Overcoming Resistance

## Resistance from Inside

If you decide to pursue the exercises in "How To Be Your Own Best Theorist II" (Hunt & Gow, 1984), let me offer some suggestions.

### Send Your Critic Away

Each of us has a part which judges, evaluates, sets standards, and criticizes. Spend a little time becoming aware of your "Critic," perhaps giving your sub-personality a name so that it will remain under control. Then arrange it so that your Critic will take some time off while you begin with yourself. Send your Critic off on a trip—maybe to a Critics' Convention—with the understanding that it will return and go back to work for you again.

### Don't Worry About "Going Public"—Write for Yourself

Initially think about beginning with yourself as a completely self-indulgent hobby, one that will be fun and exciting. Try it on for size—for your eyes only and see how you like it. If you and another colleague are mutually agreeable, then later you may begin to work with a partner. My advice, however, is to spend time with yourself at first to get over the initial resistance. Self-awareness need not be self-disclosure.

### Try to Bring Out What Is, Not What Should Be

You are the only person who truly knows your own beliefs and theories, so don't try to fool yourself. Try to develop your "Fair Witness" to help keep you honest. Engage in dialogue with yourself, asking, "Come on! Who are you kidding?"

### Remember, Self-Knowledge Is a First Step Toward Change

When you find yourself resisting because you don't like what you are bringing out, remember that you can choose to change what you do not like. Many practitioners find that the major value of beginning with themselves is to identify areas for development and change.

Teachers and Counselors

### But Remember, the Decision to Change Is Up to You

When you have brought out your ideas, you may be satisfied with them and feel good about your experienced knowledge. In this case, there is no need to change. Even if you are dissatisfied, you don't have to change immediately; the time may not be right for change. The main thing is to remember that the choice is up to you.

## Resistance from Outside

Obstacles from Outside usually arise when you begin to plan the next step in acting on the basis of your self-knowledge. In my classes we usually spend the last week discussing the problems of "re-entry" and possible resistance. We often structure this by asking "What will have to happen if . . . ?" A few suggestions from these discussions follow.

### Build a Network of Collegial Support

Beginning with ourselves can become contagious if conditions permit. The teacher centers in England are clear examples of informal arrangements that are by-and-large for the practitioners, and they embody the spirit of the Inside-out approach. My experience in creating a climate in which practitioners can share their implicit theories has demonstrated how such sharing supports, authenticates, and extends beginning with ourselves.

### Help Your Students/Clients Begin with Themselves

As I discuss in Chapter 8, the spirit of beginning with ourselves is the basis for more open, reciprocal relations between teacher and student, counselor and client.

### Arrange Your Working Relationships to Maximize Flow of Resources

Viewing every other person as a potential resource is a powerful idea, for it not only increases the overall resources available (if you are a classroom teacher) but also frees you from the personal responsibility of providing unlimited resources.

# 5
# Consultants and Supervisors Begin with Themselves

This chapter is written for those concerned with the training and professional development of practitioners: educational consultants who work with teachers, supervisors who work with therapists and counselors, and trainers who work with business personnel. Almost all consultants have been, and in many cases continue to be, practitioners who work directly with clients. Therefore, all of the ideas and methods in Chapter 4 may be applied to their work, which might be termed *primary* practice. This chapter is concerned with consultants' bringing out their implicit theories of consultation in working with practitioners, or *secondary* practice.

Distinguishing primary practice—working with students/clients—from secondary practice—working with practitioners—is essential because the way in which consultants work directly with practitioners mirrors how practitioners work with clients. For example, questions which arise include "Do consultants hold the same implicit theories in their consultation as in working directly with clients?" Or, more specifically, "Do educational consultants work with teachers in the same way they work with students, or in the way that they expect teachers to work with students?" Another issue involves the relationship between effective practice and effective consultation: "Is an excellent practitioner likely to be an excellent consultant and vice versa?" Therefore, consultants may become their own best theorists in two ways: (1) as practitioners working directly with clients

(Chapter 4) and (2) as consultants working with practitioners, as described in this chapter.

I begin with "The Problem of Three Populations" (Hunt, 1977a), then briefly discuss how actions speak louder than words in consultation through the exemplification principle. Next, I describe two consultants' implicit theories in detail and give examples of consultant's metaphors. Finally, I offer a framework for identifying patterns of consultation and outline some ways in which consultants experience and overcome resistance.

## The Problem of Three Populations

The dual role of consultants can be depicted as shown in Figure 5-1 (Hunt, 1977a).

**Figure 5-1**

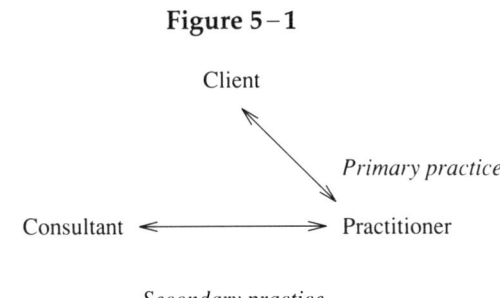

Note that the three roles in the triangle may differ: educational consultant-teacher-student; supervisor-counselor-client; or industrial trainer-manager-employee. The triangular scheme might also be applied to the preservice training of practitioners: preservice instructor-teacher/counselor trainee-student/client. In addition, this scheme provides the basis for considering the role of the theorist/researcher in relation to practitioners in Chapter 6, in which the three parties are researcher-practitioner-client.

Although the triangular scheme seems simple, it is rich with implications for understanding practice and how to improve it. For example, Elliott (1976) emphasized that each of the three parties has a different viewpoint about the same event, so he recommended "triangulation," which takes into account how a consultant, a teacher, and a student each perceive classroom events.

Figure 5–1 can also serve to describe different interaction patterns between consultant and practitioner: observation, demonstration, and discussion, as shown in Figure 5–2.

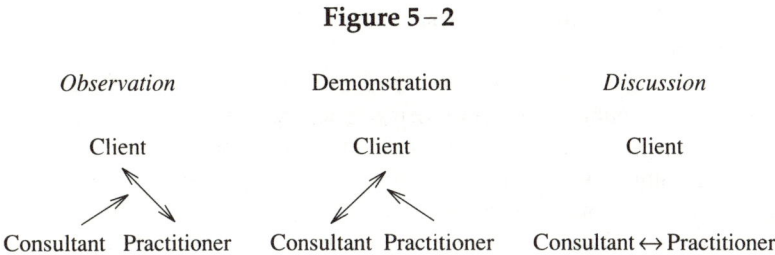

**Figure 5–2**

The three patterns are frequently called "watch them," "show them," and "talk with them," to build a framework for identifying patterns of consultation.

# Actions Speak Louder Than Words: The Exemplification Principle

This stinger, "Actions speak louder than words," is probably true in most human affairs, but it is essential for practitioners, who live in a world of actions where nothing else counts. Effective teaching, counseling, and psychotherapy all consist of skilled performance in the actions of the practitioners. Therefore, consultants, in trying to improve practitioners' skilled performance, must honor the primacy of action in practice and respect the primacy of action in their consultation with skilled practitioners.

Practitioners' responses to consultants' communications on improving practice are apt to be similar to their responses to advice on how to live their lives. That is, like the rest of us, when receiving advice from others they pay more attention to what they themselves see than to what they hear. How practitioners experience consultants' communications, attitudes, and actions in the moment is vital and, unless consultants exemplify their beliefs in their actions, their suggestions will fall on deaf ears. The way in which this *exemplification principle* works is described in communicating my ideas of "reading" and "flexing" through my actions in Chapter 2.

It is tempting to equate exemplification with modeling, in which the consultant simply demonstrates for the practitioner, but exemplification is more than simple modeling. It refers to *all* actions of the consultant—observation and discussion as well as demonstration. Modeling involves only a mechanical behavioral sequence that practitioners are expected to mimic; exemplification embodies all the actions of the consultant, which come from underlying beliefs about the nature of consulting.

Good consultation requires consultants who are skilled practitioners. Effective consultants communicate both their respect for practice as well as their own skilled performance in practice. An experience during one of my courses helped me see the truth of this statement. About halfway through my learning styles class, one of my student-colleagues said: "This class seems to be worthwhile, but I had to wait a while to decide. Whenever I take courses or workshops on teaching, I never take the teachers seriously until I have observed how they teach for a while and decided whether they know how to teach. If they seem to be good teachers, then I decide to listen. If they are not, it's all over and I tune out." I was grateful for this colleague's candor, which not only rang true but also provided me with a continuous challenge: to practice what I preach whenever I work with practitioners.

When consultants practice what they preach they speak through their actions, an approach that seems an obvious one. Yet how many of us have attended professional talks or workshops in which the speaker exhorted, recommended, and distributed materials, using actions that, as examples of practice, were completely the opposite of what was being recommended? The extreme example is the keynote speaker who urges the several hundred teachers in the audience to personalize their teaching so it will have individual meaning to individual students.

## A Consultant Brings Out Her Theories

When consultants bring out their implicit theories, their concepts turn out to be based on those they work with in their consulting—experienced teachers, counselors, or other practitioners—rather than on their students or clients. One of my student colleagues, Maureen Lanois, has given me permission to share her implicit theories, much as Jane Gow did in Chapter 4. In addition to her letter "About My Work"; concepts about clients, goals, and approaches; matching models; matching metaphor; and model of teaching development, this section concludes with excerpts from her journal, which express some of her thoughts and feelings during the process of bringing out her implicit theories.

## About My Work

Sometimes it is difficult to recognize your own teaching style unless someone else points out its characteristics to you. In this case then, I will begin by describing my own style the way my superintendent described it to me: "motherly." That label certainly makes me want to examine my own teaching more closely!

Now that I am working primarily with other teachers, my methods have changed somewhat. For "motherly," I now strive to be "unintimidating," but this is not really hard for me. Actually, I am impressed by the high level of competence and care that so many of my colleagues have, so I have as a goal to help them recognize their own potential. I try to glean *their* ideas and let them talk out an issue that concerns them. At times I admit it is necessary for me to bite my tongue, but I try to cover touchy issues with a sense of humor and keep things in perspective, and all channels of communication open.

It is also necessary to be very organized.

## Reflections About Writing Letters

Am I describing what I am, or what I hope I am? I do not really enjoy self-revealing exercises—for example, I'll never get my handwriting read. Nor do I ever "let go." The reason I am able to write this is because I took a course where journal writing was required—so this was a great help. Hopefully, it will also help me with the "reflections on the rest of this term's work."

The letter-writing format is most suitable for me, as I am beginning to find journal writing a way of "unwinding."

## My Concepts of Teachers, Goals, and Consulting Approaches

My concepts of teachers, goals, and consulting approaches are outlined in Table 5–1.

## My Matching Model

*P-E Relations*

    If a teacher characteristic is positive and shows potential, then expanding (#1, 2, 7, 9)

    If negative and confining, then focusing (#2, 6, 8)

    If misdirected or insecure, then molding (#4, 5, 10)

*P-B Relations*

    If a teacher characteristic is positive or caring, then reinforcing (#3, 4, 7, 9)

    If shows potential and is positive, then enhancing (#1)

    If negative and destructive, then modify (#2)

    If fearful, then supporting (#6, 8, 10)
              encouraging

    If undirected, then molding (#5)

*Reflections*

I wondered if at first I was just going through an exercise in semantics, but once I had these matching models completed, I could see that many of the Ps and Es could in fact be logically grouped together. Overall, it is important for me to note that none of the Es were negative.

## My Metaphor

My matching metaphor was something that struck me personally when I first read it: Shel Silverstein's "Melinda Mae" (the little girl who ate the whale); I can really relate to Melinda! Although I think of the poem in terms of learning, she also approaches all tasks—including teaching—in the same way.

    Tiny I'm not, but I'm the youngest in a large family, and was never considered quite capable or grown-up enough to take on the world!

    Monstrous whale (destroyed by eating! That's appropriate!)—a great big, shapeless job that seems almost impossible to tackle.

    Thought she could—no one else did though! I had three children under 5 when I made the decision to return to school.

    She said she would—through grinding teeth.

    Described perfectly by Shel Silverstein in *Where the Sidewalk Ends*:

## Table 5–1
## Concepts of an Educational Consultant

| | Teacher Characteristics (P) | Goals (B) | Consulting Approaches (E) |
|---|---|---|---|
| 1. (1)4(8) | Great potential for administration | Develop leadership skills | Give staff presentations, workshops, etc. |
| 2. (2)5(9) | "Boss" in classroom | See each child as an individual, not as "them" | Point out child who seems to have good rapport with the teacher as opening to discussion on other children who do not |
| 3. (3)(7)10 | Gentle | Recognize importance of being approachable by children | Comment on improvement made by "problem" child |
| 4. (4)(6)11 | Interested in trying new ideas | To plan thoughtfully | Develop methods of evaluation to make sure that new ideas are not simply "fads" |
| 5. (1)5(12) | Always looking for new methods | To evaluate methods carefully | Approach new methods with caution to make sure they are really worth trying |
| 6. (2)6(9) | Isolated from rest of staff | Be more comfortable working with others | Plan a unit of study with another staff member |
| 7. (3)(4)10 | Confident with own methods | To continue to grow in confidence | To encourage them to become associate teachers |
| 8. (5)6(11) | Fearful of change | To be more open to new approaches | Be aware of what is good in own teaching methods |
| 9. (7)(8)9 | Carefully planned lessons | To recognize value of thoughtful planning | To share lesson plans (and planning) with others |
| 10. (10)(11)12 | Insecure with own judgment | Become more self-assured | To contribute to group discussions, workshops |

### Melinda Mae

Have you heard of tiny Melinda Mae,
Who ate a monstrous whale?
She thought she could,
She said she would,
So she started right in at the tail.
And everyone said, "You're much too small,"
But that didn't bother Melinda at all.
She took little bites and she chewed very slow,
Just like a good girl should. . . .
. . . And in eighty-nine years she ate that whale
Because she said she would! (Silverstein, 1974)

## Restatement

About my work—"Motherly" is beginning to make more sense. It isn't an apple pie issue after all. While reading *Personality Structure and Learning Style* (Lawrence, 1982), it struck me that if my dominant process is "thinking judgment," that is more like earth ("earth mother"??) than sensing (water), intuitive (air), feeling (fire). (Motherly solid? Predictable? There when you need her?)

## My Model of Teacher Development

As a teacher who has been trained to work with children, finding myself now working with adults has made it necessary for me to readjust my approaches to teaching.

I recognize that children are immature and in need of a responsible adult to help them in their learning, but what about co-workers? How can I recognize their needs? How do I match my "E" to their "B"?

Some teachers want the hands-on, practical help; others are ready to take advantage of a more theoretical approach. It might be appropriate to group these teachers as to their needs in order to prepare for in-servicing next year. Even if I am not able to provide the in-servicing, I hope I will be able to suggest how/where they might obtain it.

Intuitively, I look at some young, floundering teachers and feel they'll be just fine, but in other classrooms I wonder about experienced teachers who still request the servicing of a "non-experienced survivor."

By preparing the chart, I can see links between stages which I will hopefully be able to use to help a teacher continue to develop. For example, examining appropriate methods of evaluation might be one way in which a

## Table 5-2
## Developmental Model of an Educational Consultant

| Teacher Characteristics (P) | Learning Outcomes (B) | Teaching Approaches (E) |
|---|---|---|
| help in present<br><br>"survival" | • to handle the "present" successfully without being overwhelmed by the realities of teaching | • in class help & assistance with survival techniques<br>• support & encouragement readily available |
| non-experienced<br><br>"consolidation" | • to feel more comfortable and competent<br>• to examine teaching methods with insight | • work with other teachers in school (provide opportunities for this to happen)<br>• more in-class help & assistance, especially when new approaches are being tried<br>• discuss effectiveness of new methods—especially their motivation |
| experienced survivor (knows he will make it, ready to re-evaluate position, methods, etc.)<br><br>"renewal" | • to begin to use more sophisticated and appropriate methods with class<br>• to share professional growth with others (e.g., "networking") | • examine methods of *evaluation*<br>• workshops on particular approaches to classroom learning and management<br>• find new ideas from journals, magazines—to be more selective<br>• arrange visits to other classrooms |
| "professional"<br><br>(ready to look at education from a deeper, perhaps more theoretical perspective) | • to provide a help and model to less experienced teachers<br>• to share their methods and insights with others | • share ideas and sources of ideas<br>• encourage them to take courses, seminars, leadership roles<br>• allow teachers to visit their classrooms |

teacher might begin to look at more sophisticated and appropriate methods in their classrooms.

I feel that visiting other classes will develop a spirit of professionalism and a realization that the teacher is not alone—others too are experiencing the same struggles.

In the next year, I hope to expand and develop this chart to include specific ideas and approaches I can use. To me it is logical and orderly—I hope to be able to put my finger on a problem or a desired outcome—or a teaching approach to make my in-servicing more effective—and I think I'll add another category for principals.

\* \* \*

It is important that teacher- and consultant-in-relation share their intentions. As a consultant, I do not present myself as an "expert," but rather as someone who can help teachers become aware of what they do and why.
—*Inservice Training as Persons-in-Relation* (Hunt, 1978c)

[Table 5-2 shows Maureen's model of teacher development. Bringing out such a complex model requires not only experienced knowledge but also time. The time seems well spent when the benefits of her model are considered. It provides an excellent model for her to use as an action guide in her consulting; it provides a valuable model for her consultant colleagues; and, as noted in Chapter 4, it as at least as valuable, if not more so, than any of the formal views of teacher development. Maureen also kept a journal of the *process* by which these theories came out, and these reflections—especially the many questions that she raised along the way—portray more fully the meaning of bringing out one's theories.]

## Becoming My Own Best Theorist

Some excerpts from Maureen's journal on the road to "becoming her own best theorist" follow.

**Day 1:** The first assignment demands that I look at my own work. I would really like to get a handle on that! I also feel a need for some evaluation from the teachers and principals with whom I work, because it has been a year of "experiment" for me. I feel that I'm expected to be an expert—but I'm not!! This is one of the reasons for feeling uncomfortable during those "introduce yourself" sessions. I feel that with this group. I think it will be

# Consultants and Supervisors

more of a problem of keeping up. What a knowledgeable and experienced group!

**Day 2:** The exercises make more sense now that I've had a chance to read the articles, especially "Theorist II." I am still concerned with the accuracy of my perceptions; however, I'm assured that this matter is unimportant at this time. What are others' perceptions of me?

I'm going to continue focusing on working with other teachers. I want to concern myself with how I might help them in developing and streaming their potential already in place.

In the mini-exercises, I am constantly omitting to deal with one teacher. I haven't really thought about how I can work with her. She is so defensive and abrupt, but she is still one of *my* teachers.

**Day 3:** How strongly must the P be kept in mind in our educational system? Should we mold the P to the ideals expressed in the B? Should the B be molded to the P? Should we? *Could* we? In doing a series of staff presentations, I know I change my approach according to who the Ps are. (It's also called survival.) I know what will appeal to some staffs, but not to others. I haven't figured out why there are such wide discrepancies in "staff personalities." We all share common aims and somewhat similar values (I think) but some are so difficult. Past experiences? Peer pressures? Cliques? I don't know. Perhaps there is a mismatch in some circumstances. Sometimes the teacher/instructor might not be capable of carrying out an appropriate teaching approach (e.g., does not have a dramatic flair).

**Day 4:** Small group discussion: I find I am still concerned with the assignments: Did I do this one accurately? Mine doesn't look like the others at all. I still need that strong sense of organization. The group also found that it was difficult to differentiate or consider the B and the E without considering one to the other. I'm also concerned that looking at the summary may be becoming an exercise in semantics. Have I chosen an exact enough word? Much might be left out or added to the meaning of the word.

**Day 5:** Elements of teachers' personalities which haven't seemed to come up so far: (1) Sense of humor would seem to be an important factor as to how a person handles problems. (2) Self-motivation: Personally, I panic to the point of physical discomfort when given an assignment. I am driven to get at it right away, explore *every* avenue and stick with it until it is done. And it *must* be done well before any due date. I am *very* hard on everyone around me while taking courses.

**Day 6:** Small group discussion—looking at the effect of labeling students (by fitting them into a P category). Do we limit our perspective by looking at one characteristic only? For example, if one in the group has a good sense of humor, our appeal to him would probably be very different from how we would work with the others. Does our label make the child more accessible to us? Is it better to leave some characteristics implicit instead of making everything so cut-and-dry explicit?

**Day 7:** The B-P-E diagram also helps you to recognize that you may or may not be actually doing what you *think* you are doing.

**Day 8:** How accurately can we see ourselves? Ask an observer? Tape our lessons? Do some clinical analysis? I learned a great deal from *doing* pattern analysis and it is all really tying in to this class for me now, because it is such a revealing and honest way of looking at exactly what goes on in the classroom.

When teachers produce their long-range plans over the summer, they are in fact expected to mold the "B" and the "E" without knowing the "P." Now that is pretty backward—and every teacher knows that. It certainly doesn't make the situation very flexible once those plans are submitted to the principal's office.

In providing for individual differences, an experienced teacher can provide so much in subtle ways: a knowing glance to a child who is really on the verge of a breakthrough, a touch on the shoulder that says "I understand" or "Keep it up," positioning yourself near an incident *before* it happens....

**Day 9:** I did not really realize the impact of making the teachers the "experts" until these workshops were over. I should have known if I stopped to think about it. Anyway, it certainly influences my goals and approaches for next year as I start preparing for in-service with intermediate teachers. I've got to find a way of using *their* actual lessons to share with others....

# A Trainer Brings Out Her Theories

Another colleague, Barbara Rosen-Schreiber, a trainer who works directly with older persons and gives workshops for other trainers, has agreed to share her implicit theories in print.

## About My Work

I try to make the content relative to those in the class when preparing how to do the session. If possible, I have them interact with each other—sharing experiences or doing an exercise. Although I go into a class with a fairly detailed outline, I do try to be as flexible as possible in order to best meet the needs of those involved.

# Consultants and Supervisors

I like to take the attitude that I can learn as much from them as they can from me, so I encourage questioning and group discussions. (Sometimes I'm not able to control this, in that a participant might go off on a tangent and I feel this detracts from the "lesson" I had intended to present, but I'm starting to learn that I can always give a handout which contains the desired information, and can let the session go more freely.)

## My B-P-E Concepts

Table 5-3 (see page 99) contains B-P-E concepts.

## My Matching Model

My teaching approaches can be grouped into three main categories:

1. If a positive client characteristic is recognized, I set up an environment that will *encourage* the expression of that behavior, with the hope that others will gain from it as well.
2. When a characteristic is strong, i.e., "intense," "introverted," my teaching approach is aimed at *balancing* out that characteristic, i.e., making it less intense and more easy-going, or helping an individual become more sociable if she/he is introverted.
3. I rely heavily on the use of *feedback*—both from myself and from others in the group, to help individuals become more aware of their behavior.

An underlying theme common to my P-E relations is that they are learner-centered. Very little input in terms of a discourse comes from me. This is a deliberate approach that reflects my philosophy about learning from others. I believe that everyone has something they can teach others and we can all learn from one another. Inherent in this philosophy is the notion that learning is enhanced by interacting with others.

## My Metaphor

My matching metaphor is that of beams of light, crossing and not connecting. When they do connect (when I am able to get my message or lesson across to the participants), an explosion of "insight" or awareness results (likened to a volcanic eruption) not only affecting the source of the explosion but everything surrounding it. Implicit in this metaphor is that everyone has an internal core of knowledge or awareness that is often hidden under the surface, and that once it is tapped, it can then be released.

*and that everyone contributes*

# Consultants Bring Out Their Models and Metaphors

The following matching model shows how much can be compressed into four short sentences.

1. If I have trouble relating to a teacher, I concentrate on proceeding slowly to build a relationship and modeling—vs. open feedback.
2. I give open feedback re: teaching skills to "open" instructors who are receptive to me as a person and to my ideas.
3. I do not focus on strengths but on areas to be improved.
4. If they initiate, I respond to their expressed concerns.

Following are several metaphors brought out by consultants, supervisors, and trainers. Imagine yourself in a group with these consultants and that their metaphors are available to you as a resource for your own concerns in your work. Also, imagine that you have a preview of the CREATE cycle presented in Chapter 8.

> In the imagery exercise I recreated the scene of teaching 25 adult clinicians in a three-day workshop. The image of a dance emerged. At first people shuffled and were embarrassed and there were awkward movements. I led, urged, coaxed, and repeated a few steps. The colors were red, brown, and orange. Gradually the movements of the people in the group became fluid and unified. I felt there was a blending, although not a melding. The fluidity gradually led to a feeling of soaring, flying, and swooping, with the colors of blue and white. It was very quiet. I had some fear that we would not know how to land, and that we would not want to land. My rational observer side was also in the image. It wondered about the purpose of the exercise: Were my feet on the ground? Was I being paid to dance? The confirming parts of this image were the strong and happy feelings, as well as the joining together of people. I was not at the center, nor at the head, except near the beginning and at the end.

*  *  *

> The guided imagery exercises that were conducted in class were most enjoyable! I had not experienced such an exercise before, and found that the metaphors came easily, and their features were most recognizable. The first

# Table 5-3
## Concepts of an Educational Trainer

| | Client Characteristics (P) | Learning Outcomes (B) | Training Approaches (E) |
|---|---|---|---|
| 1. (1)4(8) | intense | adopt a more relaxed, easy-going attitude | participate in "fun" events keep in touch with how you feel when doing it |
| 2. (2)(5)9 | introverted | get more involved | in partners: introduce yourself to partner, partner introduces you to group |
| 3. (3)(7)10 | attention seeker | develop sensitivity toward others | assume a role different from original behavior, later reflect on and discuss experience |
| 4. (4)6(11) | good sense of humor | encourage others to express humor | each person in group tell something humorous that happened to them (Have #4 and #11 begin) |
| 5. 1(5)(12) | supportive | to continue their helping behavior | use these two as a positive example of helping behavior |
| 6. (2)(6)9 | self-pity | learn how to like and accept self | in partners: tell person 1 characteristic you like about self and about other person—change partners at least two times |
| 7. 3(4)(10) | aware of capabilities and needs | help others set appropriate goals | reveal ways they meet goals; goal-setting exercise |
| 8. (5)6(11) | independent | continue with independent behavior and encourage others to do the same | give positive feedback when exhibit independent behavior |
| 9. (7)8(9) | very vocal (overbearing) | learn how to relinquish "control" of group | encourage group to give feedback about # of times either one initiates or dominates discussion |
| 10. 10(11)(12) | determined | continue with determination, help others develop similar attitude and behavior | create situation that allows 2 to demonstrate their determination to others |

metaphor emerged when we were asked "to go into a meadow with our colleagues." My metaphor appeared as a swirling white vapor trail that circled clockwise over the collection of people as we sat talking. It began as a trail that rose from the center of the group, and its movement was steady and equal, and in no way hypnotic, as I would have expected a swirling mass to be. The metaphor very aptly demonstrated the exchange that was occurring in the meadow, with each person contributing to that cloud and its movement. No one person contributed more, or didn't contribute at all. The contributions from each were strong and valid, and kept the vapor trail moving effectively above us. That is indeed how I perceive team meetings and case conferences to be, as we try to deal with the needs of exceptional children at the pre-referral level. Each member of that team has vital information to share, and very infrequently should any one person have power over another, or others.

My second metaphor came to mind after we had completed our matching models. The image in this exercise was of a very muscular man, who was obviously healthy and strong. The image was no doubt the result of my tossing these phrases about in my mind: "strengthen by expanding," "maximize strengths," "utilize strengths," and "provide structures to facilitate growth." When I consider my clients, indeed the goal is to make them as strong and as well-rounded (both cognitively and at an affective level) as is possible, to allow them to then act as advocates for our exceptional students. It does require considerable stamina and inner strength to break down the barriers at times.

\* \* \*

For many weeks I couldn't find a metaphor for matching. I could find one which represented me-as-teacher, that being running, but running is a solitary activity and couldn't express the interactive nature of matching. Then in early September I went sailing with my father-in-law and there it was. We experienced many wind and weather changes that day and were exhausted when we came in. He said, "Whew! That was harder than work, eh?" and as I heard myself respond, I realized sailing was an appropriate metaphor.

I, the teacher, am the sailor. I come to the boat prepared with technical knowledge, a certain fitness level, proper safety equipment and adequate provisions, as does every sailor. My student is the boat. Before we begin to sail (learn) together the boat has been built to be balanced, sleek, and seaworthy. Its designers have fitted it with sails which maximize its speed and maneuverability. At the beginning of each season one tunes the boat, testing the more or less permanent features—spars and rigging—to determine what a winter in drydock may have done, and to match them to new or recut sails. The wind is the environment. It is constantly shifting, always capricious. A helmsman must watch and listen for the slightest riffle in the sail, be aware of cloud formations and water changes, and constantly readjust if he wishes to hold his course.

There is no thrill like the perfect match of wind and boat for the sailor. The sense of being lifted slightly out of the water and transported silently through the air is magical. And often impossible to anticipate. So it is with teaching. Getting from A to B is a relatively perfunctory exercise, but finding oneself suddenly at full speed with all sails set perfectly is unintended positive learning, and requires the correct interaction of all components within a given moment.

I'd like to extend the metaphor to sail racing, which is even more exciting, but it has one inappropriate component—competition. The burden of competition makes for faster sailors but in competition the sailor pushes the boat hard and tries to control every environmental factor. He often takes risks that may damage the craft and the crew. Touring is more appropriate to my style.

\* \* \*

One metaphor that may apply to my situation is that of trying to construct a very difficult puzzle. I have all the pieces but they are scattered about in random order. I also have the picture on the box to illustrate what it is supposed to look like when it is completed. However, I don't know which piece to begin with and I don't have any guidelines as to where to start.

A maze metaphor also applies. You are in the right place and you know that there is an end point, but you have no idea which path to take.

Somehow these metaphors came fairly easily and the process helped to create a visual image in my mind of my reactions to the exercise.

\* \* \*

The metaphor I came up with in the first guided imagery exercise was a cybernetic loop, in which the teacher and child both input and receive from each other and then respond based on this interaction. Ideally, this is carried out in a relaxed atmosphere which allows for non-threatening, honest interaction to occur in both directions. The teacher watches and listens to the child and then plans subsequent action, followed by listening and watching again, etc. In reality, however, this is carried out in a highly charged, busy, active environment so it is like an electrical cybernetic experience.

\* \* \*

The matching metaphor which came to mind during the guided imagery session was that a teaching-learning experience was like an unexplored pathway of adventure. The imagery included a tour guide who, with his fellow hikers, explored the rolling, green mountainous countryside. At the summit of each ascent, new vistas would appear. Wonder, awe, and surprise were expressed by the participants.

Who is the teacher, who is the learner—for both the guide and the group experienced the sensations and discovery? When I entered into dialogue with the guide, he didn't have all the answers to my questions.

Perhaps he purposely kept from giving answers or he really didn't know what lay ahead.

The imagery is similar to working with open-ended activities which can lead to a whole range of possibilities. They do not culminate in one right answer; rather, teacher and student participate in the discovery.

\* \* \*

Finding a metaphor did not happen for me until we did the fantasy trip of twilight imaging in class. What came into my awareness was the image of the author—working with a group of researchers, developing ideas, and compiling a book or manual. Almost like a "how to" book. This metaphor relates more to what I do with the information or lecture aspect rather than the ongoing development of my staff once the information has been received. I see the latter more as nurturing—a social worker in industry, finding and providing support while developing potentials.

# Identifying Patterns of Consultation

Hookey (1985) has recently extended the triangular scheme for consultants to characterize their patterns of consultation as well as to negotiate with their clients about how they will work together. Table 5–4 is a compressed summary of the different consultant-client relations. It can serve to map the sequence of consultation over time.

# Consultants' Experiencing and Overcoming Resistance

Because consultants are also practitioners, the suggestions at the conclusion of Chapter 4 are appropriate for them. In addition, consultants must consider two basic questions: What is the meaning of being asked for help and of giving *help* in each setting? Who is the expert?

The word "help" is similar to an interpersonal inkblot in that it evokes a wide variety of interpretations. Consultants should take this inkblot test for themselves (how do they interpret "giving help"?) and for practitioners (what is the meaning of their requesting help?). For some practitioners, requesting help means admitting inadequacy, while for others it means a first step in sharing

## Table 5-4
## Patterns of Educational Consultation

1. Discussion
    a. Directed by consultant
    b. Directed by teacher
    c. Reciprocal

2. Participative teaching
    a. Consultant directs teacher and students in activity
    b. Teacher directs consultant and students in activity
    c. Consultant and teacher direct students together

3. Observed teaching
    a. Consultant teaches as teacher observes
    b. Teacher teaches as consultant observes
    c. Consultant and teacher teach part of class in view of each other

4. Supportive teaching
    a. Consultant begins, teacher follows in teaching students
    b. Consultant supports teacher in new teaching

5. Joint teaching—Both consultant and teacher teach in sequence

Source: Adapted from Hookey, 1985.

resources. Many consultants prefer to use terms other than help, such as support, assistance, or facilitation. Nonetheless, their views on providing help and on practitioners' requesting it are critical issues to confront if effective, reciprocal consultation is to occur.

An even more important term for consultants, as well as for theorists/researchers, is the word "expert." Do consultants derive their professional self-worth only from being experts who are more knowledgeable than practitioners? If so, do they see themselves as being experts both in consultation and in practice? This single word, expert, is the largest obstacle confronting consultants, theorists, and researchers in attempting to begin with themselves. Consultants must acknowledge that expertise comes from experienced practitioners (themselves and those with whom they work). Once they accept this locus of expertise, their role becomes transformed and clarified to one of (1) communicating with and relating to practitioners in a practitioner-to-practitioner equal relationship, and (2) displaying their expertise in helping practitioners bring out their knowledge and share it with others.

# 6
# Theorists and Researchers Begin with Themselves

This chapter is written for theorists and researchers in psychology and education who are interested in applying their work to practice. It is also relevant to practitioners and consultants, especially those who have temporarily become researchers in working on their doctoral theses. Since most theorists and researchers do not begin with themselves, this chapter does not contain specific examples of implicit theories like Chapters 4 and 5. Psychological theorists, such as Skinner, may write their autobiographies but they distinguish them as such from their formal theories, which are based on logic and experimental evidence rather than on personal or practical experience. Theories of psychotherapy and counseling frequently reflect the theorist-as-practitioner but theorists in other areas rarely begin by considering themselves as either practitioners or persons. Have you ever read a personality theory that began, "I grew up believing that independence and self-reliance were the cardinal virtues, and therefore those qualities stand at the top of my theory of developmental stages"?

Psychologists do not begin with themselves when they write research reports either; indeed, they do not even write in the first person singular. Have you ever read an experimental report in a journal article that began, "From my own experience, it seemed likely that there would be a relationship between a person's old, discarded role and the threat experienced from another person who exemplifies that role"? Both psychological theorists and researchers usually follow the convention of Outside-in, supporting their work by such external criteria as logic and empirical evidence rather than by the Inside-out yardstick of personal experience. For theorists and researchers to begin with themselves requires them to relinquish the role of psychologist-as-expert, the foundation of mainstream psychology. It is not surprising, therefore, that resistance from theorists and researchers is enormous, much greater than that from practitioners and consultants, because beginning with themselves requires redefining psychology and their roles as psychologists.

In making my case for an Inside-out psychology, I begin by arguing for theorist-as-person and theorist-as-practitioner, and try to show how this transition would make theorist-as-psychologist more valuable in practice and in human affairs. I illustrate this shift in role by considering two specific issues: Writing in the first person singular and accepting the possible value of common sense. I allow my Little Professor to portray Inside-out psychology in terms of the New Three Rs—Reflexivity, Responsiveness, and Reciprocality. These contrast with Outside-in of the old "UFO Model"—Unilateral, Fixed, and Objective. I illustrate how these New Three Rs guide psychological researchers, especially doctoral students, in my section *How To Be Your Own Best Researcher*.

I conclude, as usual, with a consideration of how theorists and researchers can deal with resistance to going Inside-out. I try to show, from my own experience in becoming an Inside-out psychologist, how accepting every person as a psychologist is an exciting, challenging venture, requiring more, not fewer, psychologists to help others become more self-aware and communicate more effectively.

## Theorists Are Persons, Too

Psychology is a unique subject in that the psychologists who develop the theories are also objects of study (i.e., they are participants in the human venture that they seek to understand). Obvious as this seems to non-psychologists, psychologists themselves have been very reluctant to accept the fact that they are persons, too. Indeed, it was the paper with this title, "Theorists Are Persons, Too" (Hunt, 1978a), that provoked the strong resistance described in Chapter 2.

It is equally obvious why psychological theorists resist accepting their personhood: "... in theories of human affairs, the psychological theorists can elevate their personal beliefs to the level of scientific truth" (Hunt, 1983a, p. 12). Who would want to give up such a luxury? Nevertheless, the most fundamental issue in beginning with ourselves is the psychologist's choice between psychologist-as-expert and psychologist-as-person. Mainstream psychology clings to psychologist-as-expert because this role provides control, power, and status. However, some psychologists are becoming uneasy about this false role, and a number of critiques have appeared suggesting new "paradigms."

Psychologists usually resist accepting their personhood because they believe that to do so requires them to abandon psychology-as-science. I cannot begin to consider all the complexities involved in the philosophy of science issues and will only attempt to argue directly that psychologist-as-person is an essential first step in redefining psychology. Psychologists-as-persons can certainly continue to experiment with and try to verify their ideas about human affairs, but the source of these ideas would be acknowledged for what it is—the direct experiences of persons, themselves and others.

Even though theorists may express their theories in objective terms, those who read them frequently regard these theories as representing theorists' beliefs, as indicated by the frequent use of the term "belief" in psychology textbooks (e.g. "Piaget believes that . . ."). Another illustration of psychological theories being viewed as articles of personal belief is seen in the disapproval of other psychologists when I changed my theoretical view. As I described in Chapter 2, I was viewed almost as though I had gone back on my beliefs. Textbooks may proclaim that psychological theories are open to correction, modification, and change, but when theorists actually do change their theories they are all too often seen as being unreliable, inconsistent, or hypocritical.

Nonetheless, when theorists publish their theories they do not usually acknowledge their personal beliefs or the effect of these beliefs on their formal theories. For example, in his book of interviews, *Psychologists on Psychology*, Cohen (1977) was bewildered by the disinclination of the famous psychologists whom he interviewed to acknowledge any connection between their own beliefs and their theories. As he puts it:

> One of the original aims of this book was to try and see if there was any link between the theories advocated by a particular psychologist and his own personality and motivations. . . . Few of the psychologists were very forthcoming when it came to discussing their own motivations, not so much because of reticence as because of the fact, it seemed to me, that it was *an odd question* [italics added] for them. . . . But the personality of the psychologist is, I want to argue, a very important area to investigate; for a psychologist is in a curious relation to his subject. The "subject" so-called is a person. So is the psychologist a person. (p. 9)

Most of these well-known psychologists regarded the possibility of a link between themselves as persons and their theories as an "odd question." Granted that in some areas of psychology which are remote from human affairs (such as physiological psychology), this question may be less relevant, but it is significant that the question has not been considered. I have not interviewed psychologists about this link as such, but I have noticed that some of my colleagues have strongly disagreed with my own attempts to address this "odd question."

Seymour Sarason and Dick Snow quote the reactions of their colleagues to taking seriously the complexity of human affairs and to their being personal participants in the process. Here are two responses. "I can't deal with a world where everybody has his own definition of the problem, where facts are an intrusive annoyance and of tertiary importance, where who you are is more important that what you know, and *where the need to act is more decisive than feeling secure about what the consequences will be*" [italics mine] (Sarason, 1978, p. 376). Snow's quotation of a learning theorist's response to the complexities of the teaching-learning situation is similar: "If you're right, I quit because this makes it all too complicated ... theory becomes impossible" (1977, p. 12). As shown in these quotations, which I do not think are atypical of mainstream theorists and researchers, the resistance to psychologists-as-persons runs very deep.

A part of me is not surprised at this intense resistance because I realize that mainstream psychology is built on (1) a definition of "the prediction and control of behavior," (2) the foundation of providing objective evidence for guiding human affairs, and (3) the role of psychologist-as-expert. Yet another part of me wants to shout to my colleagues about my own personal experience in shedding this role and to let them know how exhilarating it is to reclaim yourself as a person and how much more valuable you then become as a psychologist. I sometimes think of this dilemma numerically, noting that of the five billion persons in the world, there are probably no more than 100,000 psychologists. Psychologists may see psychologist-as-person as meaning they become indistinguishable from the other five billion persons, thus losing their roles and eventually their jobs. As I try to show, when psychologists reclaim their personhood and redefine psychology as a process of helping others bring out their implicit theories and facilitating communication, there will be plenty of work for them.

Psychologists are more authentic in their writing when they begin with themselves. In his otherwise excellent book, *The Reflective Practitioner* (1983), Donald Schon does not begin with himself as practitioner nor do the supervisors in the case studies begin with themselves. The credibility of Schon's proposal is accordingly limited. Similarly, one learns as much or more from reading the autobiography or biography of a psychologist [e.g., Kirschenbaum's *On Becoming Carl Rogers* (1979)] as from reading their formal theories.

# Practice Makes Perfect?
# No, Practice Makes Theory

I could have called this section "Theorists Are Practitioners Too," but I prefer the stinger "Practice makes perfect? No, practice makes theory" (Hunt, 1978b). My argument for theorist-as-practitioner is based on the same ideas expressed in Chapter 5 on the importance of consultant-as-practitioner in illustrating the Exemplification Principle. My point can be stated simply: *Unless theories come from practice, they will not apply to practice.* When practical theorists are also practitioners, both the nature of the theory and the way in which they communicate with practitioners through their actions are influenced. Let me illustrate by comparing how theorists' practical experiences have influenced the development of theories in psychotherapy and counseling as compared with the development of theories of educational psychology.

First, consider the major theories in psychotherapy and counseling: the early views of Freud, Jung, and Adler; then, later, Fromm, Horney, and Sullivan; and, more recently, Rogers, Perls, and Maslow. In every case, the theory *came from practice* and was developed by a *theorist who was also a practitioner*: Practice to theory. When theorists are also practitioners, their theories are bound to be more relevant to practice because they necessarily take into account the practical context to which they apply. Theorists' experience as practitioners also ensures that they emphasize the primacy of action in practice. Although I did not realize it at the time, George Kelly's continuing to work with clients throughout his career in order, as he said, "to keep my hand in" illustrates the theorist-as-practitioner.

Now consider the major theories of educational psychology: those of Piaget, Gagne, Bruner, Ausubel, Skinner, and so on. All these theories come from *outside* the classroom, from theorists who have not been (or who have not acknowledged being) classroom teachers. Educational psychologists are increasingly dissatisfied with the gap between theory and practice, and I believe that the major reason for this failure is that the theories have not been developed from practice. Piaget did not claim his theory was relevant to practice so, in his case, the difficulty is not with him but with others who do make such claims. Many developmental psychologists conduct "basic research," assuming that their results will automatically influence classroom practice and are frustrated when they do not. (I know, having been one of them.) Such basic research in human development and in other areas of human affairs does not influence practice because the researchers have neither acknowledged that it comes from their experience nor do they apply it to their experience. Their frustration will cease when they begin with themselves.

In the earlier consideration of theorist-as-person the question was "Do you acknowledge that your ideas come from and are influenced by your personal experience?" In the case of theorist-as-practitioner, the question is "Do you acknowledge that your ideas come from and are influenced by your practice?" That at least some educational psychology theorists regard this question as odd is illustrated in a small survey taken by Eisner (1984):

> Let me confess that I have long been intrigued about the relationship of theory to practice in education, but was motivated to write about this topic because of my experience as a faculty member at three research-oriented universities. This experience made it increasingly clear to me that research findings, and even the theories from which they are derived, seldom—indeed, hardly ever—enter into the deliberations of faculties, regardless of the area of education about which these faculties deliberate. Of course, this experience might be unique to my tenure at Ohio State, Chicago, and Stanford. Other institutions might be different.
>
> At the institutions where I have worked, questions having to do with curriculum planning, the evaluation of teaching, or the identification of institutional strengths and weaknesses are hardly ever answered in light of educational research. Thus those who are best informed about educational research seldom use the fruits of their labors either to make practical decisions or to shape institutional policy within the institutions where they work. If educational researchers do not use research findings to guide their own professional decisions, why should we expect those less well informed to use research findings to guide theirs? This anomaly and others like it moved me to raise the question that is the title of this article: Can educational research inform educational practice?
>
> Some readers may justifiably wonder if I could really know whether or not my colleagues use educational research in their own activities as teachers or as planners of curricula. Even if the fruits of educational research do not emerge in faculty deliberations, perhaps they are used by individual faculty members as they plan and teach their courses.
>
> To get answers to these questions, I asked one of my research assistants to interview faculty members in the School of Education at Stanford. The interviewees were guaranteed anonymity, and I do not know who provided which response. What I do know is that, although my colleagues in the School of Education say that they "use" research in their planning and teaching, they find it extremely difficult to give any examples of how they use it. The typical response is that research findings function in the background, as a sort of frame of reference.
>
> I suspect that my colleagues are correct, but I wonder what they mean by educational research. Altogether, I find their remarks—as reported verbatim by my research assistant—vague and unconvincing. I would hate to have to make a case for the utility of educational research in educational practice to a school board or a Congressional committee if it had to be based on statements of the kind that they provided. In addition, I collected from

each faculty member who responded to my request a copy of the reading lists and introductory course materials for the course or courses that the faculty member offered in the autumn of 1982. I examined these materials to determine whether they contained any features that might have been influenced by educational research. Did these materials contain educational objectives, for example? Alas, only the materials from one professor contained anything resembling educational objectives. Perhaps this omission is a function of the other faculty members' having read the research on behavioral objectives, but I doubt it. I use this example simply to provide what I regard as further evidence that, although we prescribe to teachers and school administrators one thing, we do another thing for ourselves. (Eisner, 1984, pp. 447–448)

To examine the way in which your theories are influenced by and continue to influence your own practice may seem odd to theorists in educational psychology, but this is not the case with theories of counseling, as Carl Rogers' development of his theories illustrates. Beginning in the early 1940s, Carl Rogers took what was in those days a radical step; he actually filmed some of his psychotherapy sessions so that what he did, rather than what he said he did or espoused, was available for practitioners to see. More than 40 years later, with all the technical advances that have been made, it is easy to dismiss the enormous importance of Rogers' bringing psychotherapy out into the open. Until he did so, theory and research in psychotherapy were based entirely on therapists' notes and recollections. With Rogers' landmark filming, he made public his theorist-as-practitioner so that his actions as well as his theories were available to practitioners.

To appreciate the significance of Rogers' filming, imagine that a similar event had taken place in educational research at that time. Suppose that a classroom teacher, Carla Rogerson, was interested in developing theories of teaching and learning and therefore filmed her own teaching as a basis on which to develop her theories. How different present-day theories of teaching-learning would be had they been initially based on actual practice. Some readers will want to remind me that we now have ethnographic approaches to classroom research in which researchers film and tape what actually occurs in order to understand classroom events, yet even now, with occasional exceptions, the theorists are not teachers. For reasons of control and power, the experienced knowledge of classroom teachers does not carry the same weight and authority as that of counselors and therapists.

# First Person Singular

In addition to bringing out psychotherapy by filming his sessions, Carl Rogers took another bold step for his time; he began to write in the first person singular, a dramatic step in the history of Inside-out psychology, as shown in his biography.

> Another change evident in *Client-Centered Therapy* was Rogers' developing personal style of communication. As a writer and a speaker he had always communicated his ideas in a clear, down-to-earth, non-esoteric manner, and in that sense he always came across as a sincere person. Having been trained in an academic setting, however, where it was proper to refer to oneself only in the third person, Rogers had followed the traditional mode for many years. "The author believes ...," "The present writer has found ...," "... explored by this investigator," would be the normal way he would insert any self-reference. Gradually he came to feel that the pronoun "I" was legitimate, even preferable in many cases. And as he began to use the first person in his speeches and writings, he became even more human to his audience. A passage from the preface to *Client-Centered Therapy* gives something of the flavor of his developing style. One editor was sufficiently surprised by this that he included the following footnote on the first page of Rogers' article:
>
>> The editor raised a question with the author regarding the frequent use of the personal pronoun in the manuscript and received a reply which deserves quoting. "The fact that it is in quite personal form is not accidental nor intended to make it a letter. In recent years I have been experimenting with a more personal form of writing for I believe that putting an article in more personal form makes it communicate more directly and, even more important, keeps us from sounding like oracles. Instead of saying, 'This is so,' one is much more inclined to say 'I believe this is so.' I just wanted you to know the reason why it is expressed in a more personal way than is considered to be good scientific writing." This argument appeared particularly to fit the nature of the article in question and the original flavor of the writing is retained.—Ed. (Kirschenbaum, 1979, pp. 169–171)

Since Rogers' breakthrough, a few editors of psychological journals now allow the use of "I," but most do not. To see the difference, consider these two forms to describe the same researcher actions: "I worked with 20 classroom teachers who had agreed to participate in my project" and "Twenty Ss were run by E." (Journalese not only prohibits the use of "I" but also prefers the passive to the active voice.) There is no clearer illustration of Inside-out vs.

Outside-in psychology than in these two examples. Consequently, all the arguments against Inside-out are bound up in objections to writing in the first person singular: non-scientific, non-objective, non-generalizable, and so on.

The resistance from Scientific Psychology to the use of "I" seems to extend beyond writing in the first person singular to the word "I" itself, as Bettelheim's description of the distorted translation of Freud's work into English illustrates. Both Bettelheim (1983) and Brandt (1983) point out that what James Strachey translated into English as the "ego" should simply have been "I," while "super-ego" should have been "above I." Bettelheim also argues persuasively that the medically-oriented American psychoanalysts preferred to distance the personal "I" to the objective Latin. For those of you who recall your first exposure to Freud's concepts of the mind, try to imagine how you would have felt if they had been "I," "above I," and "the thing" rather than the ego, the superego, and the id. It takes an expert to deal with Latin terms, but everyone understands what is meant by the "I."

## What About Common Sense?

Like writing in the first person singular, common sense poses a threat to mainstream psychology, but for a slightly different reason. If the results of a psychological experiment agree with common sense, then why bother? Imagine, for example, what would happen if common sense were used as a criterion for making decisions about which research proposal should be funded. Suppose that rather than having a committee of experts judge proposed experiments for logic and experimental design, a panel consisting of nonprofessionals (some of them "street-smart") was asked to predict the outcome of the proposals on the basis of their common sense. Would it be worth funding those experiments whose results were entirely predictable from common sense?

To use the opposite criterion—contravening common sense—would be equally problematic. Some psychologists, such as Leon Festinger, have argued for the value of the theory [e.g., *A Theory of Cognitive Dissonance* (1957)], specifically because it contravened common sense. In any case, it seems clear that the role of common sense in scientific decision making is an issue worth considering. However, as with "I," attempts to examine it are usually resisted or forgotten. For example, Fritz Heider introduces his important work, *The Psychology of Interpersonal Relations* (1958), as follows:

> The study of common sense psychology is of value for the scientific understanding of interpersonal relations in two ways. First, since common sense

psychology guides our behavior toward other people, it is an essential part of the phenomena in which we are interested. . . . Second, the study of common sense psychology may be of value because of the truths it contains, notwithstanding the fact that many psychologists have mistrusted and even looked down on such unschooled understanding of human behavior. (p. 5)

Heider then outlines a "naive analysis of action," which relies on common-sense terms such as "can," "try," and "should" rather than on psychological jargon as the basic unit of his interpersonal theory. Heider's book is frequently cited in contemporary social psychology, but only for its concept of "attribution" (a very minor part of his important theory), without referring either to his belief in the significance of common sense or to his use of common-sense terms to describe interpersonal relations. As with Freud's "I," the fact that Heider valued common sense has been "lost in translation."

In his book *Psychology and Common Sense,* Joynson (1974) is more emphatic about the necessity for psychologists to take common sense into account:

> The ability which we all have, to understand ourselves and others, presents the psychologist with a paradoxical task. What kinds of understanding does he seek of a creature which already understands itself? The psychologist has often reacted to this problem by ignoring it, or by denying that the layman's understanding need be taken seriously. But the consequences of this reaction are disastrous, and sooner or later the psychologist must face the challenge. (p. 2)

Joynson supports his contention by quoting Kohler (1947):

> The kind of experience which the layman claims to have plays hardly any explicit part in the scientific psychology of our time. I feel I must take sides with the layman; that, for once, he rather than our science is aware of a fundamental truth. For the layman's convictions are likely to become a major issue in the psychology, neurology, and philosophy of the future. (p. 323)

Bird's (1984) comments are also relevant:

> . . . everyone has assumptions about how the world works or could work. The only choice to be made is whether one will recognize, state, scrutinize, and test those assumptions or not. When persons do take care to recognize, state, examine and test their assumptions, the product tends to be called "just theory" as in the statement "That's just theory, let's get down to practical matters." . . . When assumptions are carried out in practice, they tend to be called "just common sense" as in the statement "Of course it will work, it's just common sense." (p. 77)

Theorists and Researchers 115

Joynson's and Bird's comments imply two possible answers to the question "What about common sense?" From Joynson's view, psychologists might help when the lay person finds that common sense fails. From Bird's view, psychologists might help persons bring out their theories so they could be put to the test, a suggestion that I heartily endorse.

# The New Three Rs and the UFO Model

I have been making my case for theorists and researchers to begin with themselves primarily on the basis of its intuitive appeal and its agreement with their own experience. Now I make a case using some abstract concepts and allow my Little Professor to do the talking.

"The New Three Rs" (Hunt, 1979) were originally presented as a critique on conventional research (the UFO model), and serve to depict Inside-out vs. Outside-in approaches to research in Table 6–1.

### Table 6–1

| New Three Rs | UFO Model |
|---|---|
| (Inside-out) | (Outside-in) |
| Reciprocal | Unilateral |
| Responsive | Fixed |
| Reflexive | Objective |

In this section, I change the order of the New Three Rs to form the sequence of *How To Be Your Own Best Researcher*. The order is (1) Reflexivity, (2) Responsiveness, and (3) Reciprocality.

## Reflexive vs. Objective

As George Kelly originally used it in his reflexivity principle and as I use it here, the term "reflexive" means self-reflexivity or reflecting back on oneself. Reflexivity is the first step in beginning with ourselves, an explicit bringing out of the implicit theories based on our own experience. The principle of reflexivity reminds psychological theorists that they are also objects to be understood by their own theories. In accepting the first "R," psychologists and non-psychologists acknowledge their personhood and their participation in the human venture, and reject their attempts to be detached, objective recorders of the human scene. Reflexivity goes beyond the researchers' simply labeling themselves as participant-observers—although this is a step in the right direction. Accepting the first "R" requires that the *first* thing you do is bring out your own ideas, not simply that you acknowledge them later. Accepting the first "R" does not mean that one cannot observe, only that any observation must be firmly based in one's own implicit theories and beliefs.

## Responsive vs. Fixed

An essential feature of skilled interpersonal action is responsiveness, which includes adaptability ("flexing," or "matching in the moment"). Responsiveness is the distinguishing feature in human transactions. I sometimes tell teachers that the most important quality of an excellent lesson is in its responsiveness, that is, it could not be entirely planned in advance. This second "R" can be understood as a distinctively human quality, one that no computer program will ever achieve. While science requires fixity, constancy, and consistency in its definition of a variable, the essence of human affairs lies in the "flexing" of one person to another, which sets the stage for the third "R," reciprocality.

## Reciprocal vs. Unilateral

The third "R" attempts to capture the transactional nature of human experience and results from the responsiveness of the two parties. Computer programs and some exclusively role-defined situations may be unilateral, but most human affairs are two-way encounters. Psychology borrowed the unilateral "X causes Y" scheme from the natural sciences and has been unable to relinquish it, despite its inadequacy for characterizing human transactions. In some areas, such as parent-child relations, researchers have only recently accepted the possibility of "bi-directionality of effects" (Bell, 1968), which acknowledges that the child influences the parent as well as the parent influencing the child. A similar though less successful attempt has been made to characterize teacher-student transactions as reciprocal or bi-directional (Fiedler, 1975). Everyone knows from their experience that human affairs are reciprocal, two-way encounters, yet, because this kind of relation does not fit neatly into traditional research methodology, the unilateral "X causes Y" model continues to prevail.

Each of the New Three Rs could be used to identify why there is such a large gap between research and practice, but the outmoded "X causes Y" nature of most research is probably the largest single reason for its irrelevance to practice.

# How To Be Your Own Best Researcher

In working with doctoral students (who are usually also experienced practitioners) in our psychology of teaching program on their thesis proposals, I recommend that they try to reclaim their experienced knowledge as a basis for supporting and clarifying their ideas for thesis research. Recently, I have adapted the New Three Rs for this purpose into a suggested sequence, *How To Be Your Own Best Researcher*. The following three steps are appropriate for any researcher, but I describe how they have been used by doctoral students in developing their thesis proposals and conducting their thesis research.

## Reflexivity in Research: Interview Yourself

For most doctoral students, the process of identifying a research topic and paring it down to a reasonable size is a major concern. The application of the first R, Reflexivity, helps to get the student started. The first step involves having the researcher describe the topic in ten words or less (e.g., "Introducing microcomputers into elementary classrooms," "Identifying patterns of educational consultation," or "The role of small group discussion in history classes"). When a student says, "But I don't have a topic yet," I reply, "Just imagine that you have to begin now. What would it be?" Being reflexive on any topic, whether or not it turns out to be the final choice, helps to clarify and focus one's thoughts.

Next, the researchers prepare a rough interview guide on the chosen topic, consisting of four questions [drawn from the four phases of Kolb's (1984) experiential cycle, described in Chapter 8]: (1) "What has your experience with this topic been?" (2) "From your own experience, what do you think are its most important features?" (3) "In terms of your experience with this topic, what are your hunches about how it works, i.e., how do you make sense of it?" (4) "Based on your understanding of this topic, what is the first step to take in investigating it?"

Once the interview is set, researchers find someone to interview them as they become the first participant in their research. In this reversal of roles, researchers bring out their ideas by being interviewed. They record these interviews, which bring out their present understanding of their topic. Bringing out their implicit understanding about their topic serves to (1) help them decide whether or not to pursue this topic further, (2) provide a personalized framework within which to review the work of others on the topic, (3) raise their awareness about how participants may feel so that they can be more responsive in the next phase, and (4) establish an initial understanding from which to consider how much additional insight may be gained by investigation (i.e., psychological research as increased personal understanding).

Researchers should also become participants later in their work, after they have developed their methodology and before they begin their investigation. Whether it is an experiment, questionnaire, survey, interview, or observation, they will benefit by going through the specific method as participants. As simple as this advice sounds, I have known very few researchers who have taken the time to "run themselves" as subjects. Becoming a participant in your own research project is a very valuable source of feedback for tuning into whatever methods are used—the Golden Rule in developing research methods.

## Responsiveness in Research: Listen to the Participants

The researchers' initial understanding, brought out in the first step, sets the foundation for learning more about potential participants. This phase is not to be confused with a so-called "pilot study," which usually requires gaining access and consent forms. The purpose of the second step is to inform the researcher about the views and attitudes of the participants on the topic and on participating in the research. First, identify a potential participant (e.g., if the topic is "Microcomputers in the Elementary Classroom," then find an elementary teacher). The researcher then arranges an interview with the teacher, but the purpose of the interview is *not* to negotiate participation but rather to enlist cooperation in providing information about how the teacher views research. It is vital that the researcher make clear in arranging the interview that its purpose is to obtain a description of the interviewee's previous experience with research and attitudes toward future participation.

In conducting the interview itself, the researcher explores the following issues with the interviewees: (1) "What have your previous experiences with research involved—experiments, surveys, questionnaires, or experimental programs?" (2) "Based on your earlier experience with research, what are the major issues in your participation in research?" (3) "What are your feelings and ideas about how research should be carried out?" (4) "Based on the ideas you have expressed, can you summarize the conditions under which you would be willing to participate in a research study?" (Again, the four phases are adapted from the Kolb cycle.) This step may be repeated with other potential participants, of course, and this information sets the stage for the next phase—the third "R," Reciprocality.

## Reciprocality in Research: Negotiating Participation

Researchers use what they have learned through their interviews in the first two steps to formulate some tentative conditions for negotiating participation. Although these conditions will be similar to those often formally identified in ethical guides, such as guarantees of privacy, confidentiality, and anonymity, they will likely transcend these formal concerns to include such issues as the researcher's taking the participant's views into account and allowing participants to consider the researcher's interpretation of their actions or comments. Participation is negotiated in a reciprocal fashion so that the research enterprise itself has some of the reciprocal flavor that characterizes non-research transactions.

This application of the New Three Rs may seem unrealistic and perhaps fanciful to some; I therefore conclude this section by noting that I do not insist that the student researchers who engage in this Inside-out approach write their theses in this fashion. Indeed, they may not even write them in the first person singular. What I recommend is simply that they try to go through the New Three Rs early in the process of developing their proposals, and they usually find that it gives them a foundation from which to proceed. Some researchers may choose to keep their notes entirely private, as one might keep a journal; others may choose to include part or all of this process in their thesis. Whether public or private, they have established their personal foundation. In describing *How To Be Your Own Best Theorist* in Chapter 4, I emphasized that the choice of "going public" with one's implicit theory is up to each person. The same point applies here. The choice of whether to include this process in your final research report is entirely up to you.

When I first described the New Three Rs in 1979, I was not aware of the importance of their being taken in order. However, when sequenced as Reflexivity – Responsiveness – Reciprocality, there is a natural order proceeding from self → other → mutual adaptation, as seen in Figure 6–1.

A just-completed doctoral thesis by Sharon Bray (1986) shows how a researcher's beginning with herself initiates a spirit of reciprocality. She began her research which investigated teacher thinking by videotaping her own teaching while being observed by the participants. Her Reflexivity-in-action set the stage for creating a reciprocal, trusting relationship with the participants.

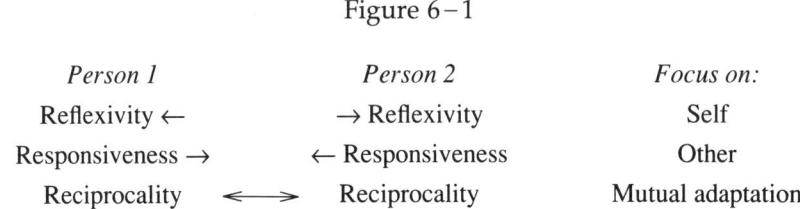

Figure 6-1

| Person 1 | Person 2 | Focus on: |
|---|---|---|
| Reflexivity ← | → Reflexivity | Self |
| Responsiveness → | ← Responsiveness | Other |
| Reciprocality  ←→  Reciprocality | | Mutual adaptation |

# Overcoming Resistance and Redefining Psychology

Throughout this chapter, I have emphasized the strong resistance from theorists and researchers to beginning with themselves; I won't repeat all the obstacles. The major obstacle for theorists and researchers is their feeling that adopting an Inside-out psychology means abandoning psychology-as-science and its related "basic research." Whether or not psychology is still a science when redefined as Inside-out depends on one's definition of science.

However, for personality, social, educational, and developmental psychologists, accepting an Inside-out psychology will mean they cannot defend their work simply because it is "basic research." When one looks at the record of the first hundred years of psychological research (excluding physiological and animal research), there are very few examples in which "basic research" in psychology has had any influence on human affairs. For theorists and researchers to begin with themselves requires nothing more or less than a complete redefinition of psychology and the role of psychologists.

In 1980 I outlined the functions of psychologists in an Inside-out psychology as follows: "(1) to help create open, reciprocal climaxes, (2) to enhance the self-knowledge of themselves and others, and (3) to facilitate communication" (Hunt, 1980a, p. 292). To these I would now like to add: (4) to test their own implicit theories and those of others.

As to specific suggestions for overcoming internal resistance, I turn again to George Kelly, who encouraged clients to try out new approaches gradually and in settings in which they are least threatened. Theorists and researchers may also try out some of these new approaches privately or under circumstances that are not threatening. If you try beginning with yourself, see how it feels and how it seems to work. It will be a gradual process and not an easy one, but then nothing valuable ever is. I hope you will give it a try and find it as exciting as I have.

# 7

# Beginning with Ourselves in Practice-Theory Relations

The relationship between practice and theory has been an important underlying concern in Chapters 4, 5, and 6, even though they focus primarily on the individual participants—practitioners and theorists. In this chapter, the relationships between practitioners and theorists—specifically, how to facilitate and sustain them—are discussed. I use three stingers introduced earlier to build my case: (1) practice makes theory, (2) practice to theory as persons-in-relation, and (3) implementation as mutual adaptation (McLaughlin, 1976).

These themes are amplified in six sections: (1) a description of images showing how practice and theory are related; (2) McLaughlin's idea of "implementation as mutual adaptation" used as the basis for summarizing what were found to be effective and ineffective implementation strategies in the large-scale RAND study (Berman and McLaughlin, 1976); (3) a continuation of this topic by examining "studies in mutual adaptation," which sets the foundation for the following section; (4) ways in which theorists can use the New Three Rs to develop reciprocal working relations with practitioners; (5) a more specific illustration of these ideas applied to staff development; and, finally, (6) a discussion of ways to overcome resistance to changing the image of practice-theory relations.

## Images of Practice-Theory Relations

### Top-Down Image

In this conventional Theory → Practice image, social scientists claim that improved practice must come from formal theories and basic research. It may take time, but when sufficient knowledge has been accumulated it will directly influence the actions of practitioners. Borrowed from natural science (however inaccurately), this one-way image typifies the unilaterality of Outside-in; theory controls practice, knowledge controls action, and mind controls body. Figure 7–1 summarizes the major features of the top-down image and the criteria for acceptance associated with each phase.

**Figure 7–1**

**Top-Down Image of the Relation Between Theory and Practice**

|    | *Phase*              | *Criterion for Acceptance*    |
|----|----------------------|-------------------------------|
| 1. | Formal theory        | Logic                         |
|    | ↓                    |                               |
| 2. | Experimental research| Validity and generalizabilty  |
|    | ↓                    |                               |
| 3. | Program development  | Clarity and organization      |
|    | ↓                    |                               |
| 4. | Implementation       | Fidelity to prescribed program|

My work on Conceptual Level Theory, summarized in Chapter 2 (1961–1971), illustrates this traditional sequence. First, the formal theory was set forth in *Conceptual Systems and Personality Organization* (Harvey et al., 1961), making its case for developmental and person-environment matching on a logical basis. Next, controlled experiments were conducted to validate these logically derived principles (Hunt, 1971). Having met the twin criteria of theoretical logic and experimental validity, the theoretical principles then provided the foundation on which to develop programs and curriculum guides (e.g., three different versions of a consumer education course were developed in Minnesota for students with three different learning styles). Finally, these programs were "delivered" for implementation in the classroom. That this "implementation," from the top down, was unsuccessful should have surprised no one since other efforts to use this top-down model had been consistently unsuccessful. What is surprising is that anyone would expect success from this sequence. Stop and think about the assumptions underlying this image and compare them with your own experience. Is it likely that the skilled performance of an experienced teacher will be greatly affected by a piece of paper? The top-down image is typified by the motto of one of the leading research institutes on teaching: "It's the thought that counts." Not so in practice: The motto should be "Actions speak louder than words."

Note that this traditional image of Theory → Practice is identical to the UFO research model. It is *U*nilateral in that it takes a one-way view of the sequence (theory + research → program development → implementation). It is *F*ixed because the sequence is inflexible and because it is unresponsive in making no allowance for feedback from practice. Finally, it is *O*bjective in that its language involves the use of impersonal abstractions (e.g., theory and implementation rather than the participating persons, theorists, and practitioners). Its language also uses the passive voice, as in the research reports (e.g., "The program is to be implemented"). Indeed, the teachers and practitioners are literally viewed as mechanical implements, evaluated by their non-responsiveness. The closer they come to resembling a computer in the perfect, inflexible execution of programs, the better the implementation. Not only are their beliefs and skills ignored in such program evaluation but also they are viewed as non-responsive machines "delivering" programs.

Am I exaggerating? You may hear yourself saying, "Wait a minute . . . the days of the teacher-proof curriculum are over." You are right if you consider the way in which new programs are evaluated today. We don't use these words anymore, but the melody lingers on. You will find this top-down image alive and well under different euphemistic labels. If you would like to check out its continuing prevalence, try to change it, as Lewin would say. Here is what I did. Although the journal *Theory Into Practice* is not necessarily exclusively devoted to a top-down image, its name implies that it is. I therefore concluded the original "How To Be Your Own Best Theorist" by proposing that its name be changed to *Practice Into Theory* (Hunt, 1980a, p. 293). However, it is all too easy to dismiss even so appropriate a stinger as a mere play on words; I was therefore not surprised when my suggestion was not adopted or even considered. At least I was in good company, for in 1949 the eminent philosopher Gilbert Ryle observed that "Efficient practice precedes the theory of it" (Ryle, 1949, p. 30).

## Bottom-Up Image

If you don't like something, turn it upside-down and see how it looks. The bottom-up image (see Figure 7–2) is simply a complete reversal of top-down and, like the original, is also lopsided, although closer to the actual phenomenon:

### Figure 7–2

### Bottom-Up Image of the Relation Between Practice and Theory

*Phase*

1. Skilled performance of practitioner
↓
2. Practitioner's implicit theories
↓
3. Theorist's understanding of practitioner's implicit theories
↓
4. Research to check implicit theory

Since most of the remainder of this chapter is devoted to examining this sequence and the criteria associated with each phase, I will not elaborate on it here. For now, this reversal sets the stage for the next image.

## Back-and-Forth Image

Reversing the sequence is necessary to establish the basis for the reciprocity between practitioner and theorist in this back-and-forth image (see Chapter 2). Note also that I have changed the description from the abstract terms of theory and practice to the participating persons, practitioners, and theorists. One way to view these three images and how reversal contributes to reciprocity is to perceive them as variations of the Transactional Analysis (TA) scheme (Berne, 1964), which views the roles and role relationships between persons as combinations of three roles: parent, child, and adult. For these TA roles, I substitute theorist, practitioner, and person, respectively. I visualize the three images as shown in Figure 7–3.

In this third image, the two participants might also relate equally as theorist-theorist or as practitioner-practitioner. In all three cases, the two parties relate as equals (back-and-forth) rather than in a power hierarchy as in Theorist → Practitioner. That this reciprocal image of practitioner and theorist is more than an article of faith and, indeed, is supported by a great deal of evidence is the topic of the next section.

### Figure 7–3

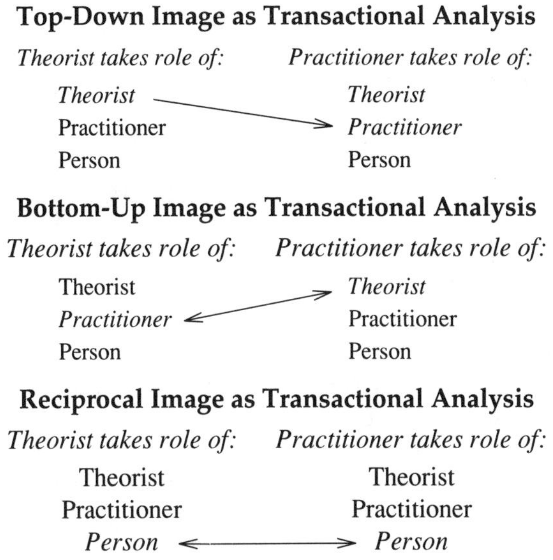

**Top-Down Image as Transactional Analysis**

| Theorist takes role of: | Practitioner takes role of: |
|---|---|
| Theorist | Theorist |
| Practitioner | Practitioner |
| Person | Person |

(arrow from Theorist [left] to Practitioner [right])

**Bottom-Up Image as Transactional Analysis**

| Theorist takes role of: | Practitioner takes role of: |
|---|---|
| Theorist | Theorist |
| Practitioner | Practitioner |
| Person | Person |

(arrow from Theorist [right] to Practitioner [left])

**Reciprocal Image as Transactional Analysis**

| Theorist takes role of: | Practitioner takes role of: |
|---|---|
| Theorist | Theorist |
| Practitioner | Practitioner |
| *Person* | *Person* |

(double-headed arrow between Person and Person)

# Implementation as Mutual Adaptation: The RAND Study

The most definitive work ever conducted in educational implementation and practice-theory relations is a review conducted by Berman and McLaughlin (1978) of numerous implementation efforts, published in their monumental eight-volume report frequently referred to as the RAND study.

The phrase "research tells us" usually refers to a few experimental studies with some tentative practical implication. But in the case of the RAND study, Berman and McLaughlin reviewed hundreds of efforts to implement educational changes costing billions of dollars, and their research tells us something very practical—what factors or combinations of factors led to sustained change and what factors did not. Table 7–1 summarizes effective and ineffective strategies taken from Berman and McLaughlin (1978).

## Table 7-1

## Effective and Ineffective Strategies

| *The following were supportive strategies, especially when applied in concert:* | *Ineffective strategies were:* |
|---|---|
| 1. Concrete, teacher-specific, and extended training | 1. Packaged management approaches |
| 2. Classroom assistance from project or district staff | 2. One-shot, pre-implementation training |
| 3. Teacher observation of other similar projects in other classrooms . . . | 3. Pay for training |
| 4. Regular project meetings that focus on particular problems | 4. Formal evaluation |
| 5. Teacher participation in project decisions | 5. Outside consultants |
| 6. Local materials development | |
| 7. Principal participation in training | |

*Source:* Berman and McLaughlin, 1978, pp. vi–ix

I hope you have noted that these two columns might have been equally well labeled "Inside-out" and "Outside-in," respectively, and of course this is one reason for my including them; how delightful to find evidence to support my beliefs! A more important reason for including the RAND results is that they must be seriously considered by anyone interested in how theory and research relate to educational practice. Because of the unprecedented scope of the RAND study, it provides the best available source on which to build an understanding of practice-theory relations. The RAND study is not just another review; it is the fundamental basis for understanding how we must proceed in improving the quality of education. It is commonplace in educational innovation to ignore results of ten years ago, but these results are not dated. Any proposal for educational innovation must come to terms with these findings, either by taking them as basic assumptions (as I do) or by providing counter-evidence that is at least as comprehensive as the original RAND results.

Practice-Theory Relations

In her paper "Implementation as Mutual Adaptation" (1976), McLaughlin summarizes the results in a mutual adaptation framework as follows:

> The adaptive implementation strategies defined by effectively implemented local projects were comprised of three common and critical components—local materials development; concrete on-going training; on-line or adaptive planning and regular, frequent staff meetings. These elements worked together in concert to promote effective implementation. Where any one component was missing or weak, other elements of the overall implementation strategy were less effective than they might be. A most important characteristic these component strategies hold in common is their support of individual learning and development—development most appropriate to the user and to the institutional setting. The experience of classroom organization projects underlines the fact that the process of mutual adaptation is fundamentally a learning process. (McLaughlin, 1976, p. 348)

# Studies in Mutual Adaptation

I encountered McLaughlin's 1976 paper two years later when preparing a proposal to study mutual adaptation, which was subsequently funded by Canada Council/Social Science and Humanities Research Council. I summarize a few of our experiences on this project because they typify the prospect and problems of initiating and sustaining the New Three Rs in practice-theory relations.

My original proposal for "Studies in Mutual Adaptation" was at once grandiose and non-specific. It was organized around the value of mutual adaptation in the classroom, in practice-theory relations, and in human affairs. I intended to investigate it at all three levels. Mutual adaptation was defined in terms of respect, acceptance of differences in others, cooperation, and reciprocality. I proposed to investigate its role in the classroom by attempting to facilitate a mutually adaptive climate through training students in listening skills and group learning. (If you want to understand something, try to change it.)

As we initiated these classroom activities and worked with teachers to bring mutual adaptation into their curriculum and classroom climates, we kept field notes to record case studies in mutual adaptation, on which to develop a framework of Practice ↔ Theory as mutual adaptation. My colleagues Nancy Watson and Mary Rosser conducted most of this essential activity. Finally (and this is the point at which my proposal became grandiose), I aimed to develop a framework for characterizing interpersonal transactions in human affairs inside and outside the classroom. (This is discussed briefly in Chapter 8.) My proposal was also the antithesis of the typical step-by-step proposal of methods and procedures because I argued that our research, like the mutual adaptation process being investigated, must be responsive and therefore could not be specifically planned in advance. You can see why I was a little surprised when it was funded.

## Initiating Collaborative Relationships

We met with several interested teachers in May 1979 to discuss the possibilities of collaboration. After describing our research proposal and outlining the training in listening skills and group learning, we distinguished our proposed work from traditional research, which sought to "get into the schools" and "run the subjects." We hoped to find teachers who shared our feelings about the value of mutual adaptation; we wanted teachers who were willing to back their values with a commitment of time and resources to infusing the spirit of mutual adaptation in their classes. After listening to each teacher's specific plans for the following year, we discussed more specifically how we might work together, adapting our plans to meet each of our intentions. These meetings led to negotiated agreements with three teachers (of English and social studies) to work together during the following academic year.

We recorded and transcribed these discussions to permit a more thoughtful consideration of the "negotiation of research," and reflection on these discussions brought out the importance of taking account of teachers' formal requirements, e.g., curriculum units and required evaluations, which are non-negotiable. Teachers have many formal requirements, actual or perceived, within which they have "wiggle room" to negotiate or to adapt in negotiating. Researchers sometimes view these formal requirements as obstacles, but as Sarason (1982) points out, professors are likely to think that classroom teachers have as much autonomy (read non-restriction) as they do in their graduate courses. We tried to understand and clarify these "non-negotiable" requirements of teachers, according them the same respect that we asked the teachers to give to our non-negotiable requirements as researchers, e.g., completing research, filing progress reports, and so on.

## Establishing New Roles in Reciprocal Relationships

It is easier to describe unproductive roles for researchers—objective detached Es who are running Ss—than to describe the new roles for researchers in a mutually adaptive collaboration.

My colleague Nancy Watson summarized her experience with several teachers and schools during the project as follows: "My role in all this could probably be described as a team worker (with the teachers), an advisor, an advisee, a reflector as well as a teacher, collector of data, and curriculum preparer" (Watson, 1982, p. 6).

Notice that she does not include the role of consultant even though it might be considered appropriate. For us, as researchers, to describe ourselves as consultants could create another problem, as we might be seen as threatening the territory of those who hold that title. As shown in the Transactional Analysis diagrams in Figure 7–3, the aim is for the practitioner-theorist to strike a relationship of equality, whether it be person-to-person, practitioner-to-practitioner, or theorist-to-theorist. To do so requires some transition in the theorist/researcher's role in the emerging working relationship. To be called a "resident-visitor," as I was at Thornlea, is not bad.

## Values and Operating Principles in the Project

In discussing possible collaboration with teachers and principals, we found it useful to summarize the basic values as well as the operating principles we adopted in our Mutual Adaptation Project (Hunt, 1980c, p. 2):

### Value Principles

1. That mutual adaptation, and its associated reciprocal relations, is a desirable goal not only for students, but for teachers and ourselves.
2. That teachers and students have valuable understandings of the phenomenon we are investigating and that their understandings should be coordinated with our own.
3. That we will best be able to incorporate such understandings by maintaining a reciprocal and open relation to teachers and to students.

These three beliefs lead to the following **Operating Principles**:

1. That teachers participate because they choose to do so after a thorough discussion with us.
2. That teachers who participate commit themselves to incorporating listening/group skills into their classroom work for at least two months.
3. That our methods attempt to take account of the perspectives of teachers and students whenever possible.
4. That our activities with teachers and students be open so that they will be aware of the goals of these activities.
5. That the school administration be supportive of the work.
6. While valuing mutual adaptation and reciprocality, it is clear that the relevance of listening/group skills varies for different subjects, topics, and objectives.

# The New Three Rs as Guides for Theorists Working with Practitioners

Using the sequence suggested in Chapter 6 for *How To Be Your Own Best Researcher,* we offer a sequence to help theorists develop mutually beneficial working relationships with practitioners by following the New Three Rs:

| | |
|---|---|
| *R*eflexivity: | Theorists become aware of themselves as practitioners ← |
| *R*esponsiveness: | Theorists listen to and try to understand practitioners → |
| *R*eciprocality: | Theorists develop reciprocal relationships with practitioners ↔ |

Of course, it takes two to develop a two-way relationship, but I direct these suggestions to theorists/researchers because it is up to them to take the initial steps. As the arrows show, when theorists become self-aware (←) and try to understand the other (→), a foundation for a two-way relationship (↔) is set. Practitioners also can follow these steps, as described in Chapter 4.

Expressing suggestions in "How to..." form has the virtue of clarifying the steps, but it also has the inherent disadvantage of becoming a recipe to be followed mechanically. Interprofessional relationships are quite unlike following a recipe for assembling a model airplane and may well defy any prescribed sequence or set rules. These three steps may be quite valuable, but they will not serve their purpose unless adopted with the underlying spirit and attitude that you want to achieve a mutually beneficial, reciprocal, and trusting relationship with practitioners. Perhaps you cannot completely embrace all of these values, but you must "try them on for size" by tentatively accepting them. Unless you do, the suggested steps are doomed to fail. Without this spirit of reciprocity, these suggestions are like skeletons, words without music.

## Reflexivity: Theorists Become Aware of Themselves as Practitioners

We know from Eisner's survey of education professors described in Chapter 6 that they are likely to regard the suggestion to adopt the first "R" as odd, but the same suggestion is really quite simple for theorists. Using your own experience as a teacher of graduate or undergraduate students or your experience in supervising thesis research, bring out your implicit theories of practice by going

## Practice-Theory Relations 133

through the *How To Be Your Own Best Theorist* exercises in Chapters 4 and 5. For example, I sometimes find it useful to identify how I supervise doctoral students through the thesis process. Using the Rep Test triadic sorting, I identify my concepts of these students and then bring out my goals and approaches in working with them. One benefit from such Inside-out exercises is to discuss with the students whether I have interpreted their preferred approaches as they see them.

How can theorists/researchers who work in university or college settings raise their awareness about their own formal requirements as teachers/practitioners so that they can better understand the requirements of classroom teachers? In the case of thesis supervision, for example, I found it very interesting to bring out the formal requirements for both the student and the supervisor. For the doctoral students who are beginning their theses, there are many formal requirements to meet. However, for university professors there are almost no explicit formal requirements as to how many or in what way they should supervise. Without debating the advisability of specifying supervision load or more detailed responsibilities of thesis supervisors, it is noteworthy that professors enjoy considerable latitude in choosing whether to work with students and how to work with students. Only the formal requirements of the students are stated.

During the writing of this book, the Toronto newspapers carried a front-page story about a lawsuit pending against Ryerson Polytechnical Institute. The student made his case on the basis that the professor did not teach the course as described in the catalog ("truth in packaging"). This is a clear, if extreme, example of a potential formal requirement in postsecondary education. I am certainly not advocating greater specification of work load, thesis supervision load, or any other requirement for professors, but I do suggest that theorists/researchers in colleges and universities consider their own formal requirements as compared to those of teachers in elementary and secondary education, where they are much more demanding and specific.

For some theorists, bringing out their implicit theories of practice may be facilitated by working with a colleague, while others may wish to bring out their implicit theories of practice in private. In either case, if theorists can cut through their resistance to this "odd question" of the relationship between their formal theories and their implicit theories of practice, they will find much value in comparing the two.

I conclude these suggestions on theorists' raising their consciousness by mixing a metaphor: By putting on their practitioner's hats, they will be better able to step into the practitioner's shoes.

## Responsiveness: Theorists Listen and Try to Understand Practitioners

Most of my suggestions for theorists to be responsive to practitioners are simply variations on the repeat and reply exercise in listening skills training. "Repeat and reply" is a special form of communication with arbitrary rules to minimize misunderstanding. For example, if I am trying to understand a practitioner's views, I must repeat, or paraphrase, what I understand the practitioner has said before I can reply. Also, my repeat or paraphrase must satisfy the practitioner as an accurate interpretation before I can reply. This exercise sounds simple, but when you try it you will find it very powerful—it is mutual adaptation in action.

In his paper "Mutual Adaptation and Mutual Accomplishment: Images of Change in a Field Experiment," Bird (1984) recommends adopting the mind-set of assuming that the practitioner's actions and views are rational and trying to learn about them:

> One of the useful reactions [in listening to practitioners] was to pretend that the other person was being rational in a way that was not immediately apparent but that might be discerned. In general, asking how an action was rational was more useful than telling how it was not. Proponents and adopters could educate each other and attempt to satisfy their different points of view. (Bird, 1984, p. 75)

It is important that the change in mind-set by the theorist include a corresponding shift in attitude so that the theorist is truly interested in and curious about the practitioner's implicit theory. Many practitioners expect theorists and researchers to be critical of their views, so theorists not only must avoid condescension and sarcasm (e.g., "Isn't that *interesting*?" spoken in a snide tone of voice) but also must go out of their way to display a non-judgmental, accepting attitude. Theorists who read about Piaget's use of clinical interviews with children to learn more about how they think are likely to applaud his skill in bringing out their ideas by being accepting and non-judgmental. Theorists need only follow Piaget's example in their communication with practitioners.

Theorists may also ask practitioners to apply a specific theoretical dimension to learn about how practitioners understand it. For example, when I was using Conceptual Level as a measure of students' need for structure I often asked teachers to rate their students on this dimension, based on their observations. Upon comparing teacher ratings on need for structure with tested CL scores, there were two results. First, teacher ratings were quite close to CL scores in most cases. When they were not, teachers were frequently rating ability rather than need for structure. Second, in other cases of disparity, I found that the CL score sometimes missed the mark in terms of how a student functioned in the social setting of the classroom. For example, some students might score fairly high on

CL because they were able to think through a problem individually, but in the classroom they could not do so without considerable teacher support.

Another mind-set for initiating and sustaining responsiveness in listening to practitioners is to think of the interchange as involving translation—that is, paraphrasing the practitioners' comments into theorists' understanding. Like the repeat and reply exercise, after the practitioner's comment the theorist says, "Let's see if I understand this. Would it be like . . . ?", making certain the practitioner would feel comfortable in correcting the translation if he feels it's inaccurate. In this mind-set, one considers practitioner language and theorist language to be different versions of reality, each to be respected and appropriate for its purposes but requiring translation if reciprocality is to result.

The "dictionary" in Table 7–2 provides a translation of research terms into practitioner language (Hunt & Sullivan, 1974, p. 263).

### Table 7–2

### Translating Psychological Terms into Educational Practice

| Psychological Idea or Term | Educational Translation |
|---|---|
| Matching | Meeting a student's needs |
| Conceptual Level (CL) | Need for structure |
| Low CL | Student who needs structure |
| High CL | Student who needs less structure |
| Variation in structure | Teaching methods |
| Paragraph Completion Test | Questionnaire |
| Developmental perspective | Providing support for growth |
| CL grouping | A way to help students become more independent and increase their self-esteem |

One result of theorists' forcing themselves to translate practitioners' ideas into terms comprehensible to themselves and to translate theoretical terms into language comprehensible to practitioners is the dejargoning of the language of theory and research. This is not a recommendation for sloppiness and imprecision but for clarity through comprehensibility. When theorists take the time and make the effort to listen and try to understand practitioners' views, the effect is bound to create more positive relationships. I learned quickly when helping persons become better listeners through such exercises as repeat and reply that being listened to carefully and sympathetically does not happen often. When it does occur, therefore, even if the listener is not highly skilled, it paves the way for a reciprocal relationship between speaker and listener.

## Reciprocality: Theorists Develop Reciprocal Relations with Practitioners

Having brought out their own intentions through reflexivity and having achieved some understanding of practitioners' intentions through responsiveness, theorists are now in a position to begin to negotiate some form of working agreement. In some cases, however, after listening carefully to practitioners, theorists will realize that time and resources to negotiate a working relationship are, at the present time, not sufficient. When we first began our Mutual Adaptation Project, for example, we talked with some of the teachers at a school in which we had previously worked. Our discussions were held in the autumn and the teachers were already committed for the year so that, although they were willing to talk, they did not have sufficient "wiggle room" to establish a working relationship. This example also illustrates the importance of who initiates the contact. When practitioners call us, we have the stated concern as a basis for negotiation; however, when we call them, reciprocity is more difficult to establish.

Theorists and practitioners may negotiate working relationships over a long period, as I did over five years at Thornlea; over a moderate length of time, as the two or three months that Nancy Watson worked on the Mutual Adaptation Project; or as a "one-shot deal," as in some professional development work. In each case, it is useful to make explicit the "unit of negotiability" (i.e., the period of time within which we will work together before reviewing our mutual accomplishments and negotiating a new agreement). These negotiated understandings are informal contracts that ensure a clear understanding of each party's responsibility as well as how we will work together. Some examples of these informal contracts are outlined in the next section.

I conclude this section with Table 7–3, which summarizes the three-step sequence involved in the New Three Rs and the criteria that must be applied to each step.

## Table 7-3

### Summary of New Three Rs Used by Theorists and Criteria for Each Step

| Step | Goal | Criteria |
|---|---|---|
| | *For theorists to:* | |
| 1. Reflexivity | Understand their own implicit theories of practice | Agreement with their theories-in-use |
| 2. Responsiveness | Understand practitioners' implicit theories of practice and formal requirements | Practitioners' agreement on theorists understanding |
| 3. Reciprocality | Develop and sustain a reciprocal relationship with practitioner | Negotiated agreement of understanding acceptable to both parties |

# Beginning with Ourselves in Staff Development

Nowhere is one's image of the relationship between practice and theory more important than in staff development, the process by which experienced practitioners affirm and extend their experienced knowledge and skilled performance. The activities in this process may be called in-service training, continuous education, or professional activity, but I prefer the term "professional renewal" because it implies a continuing process and the probability of reciprocality. In the following pages I apply many of the themes from this chapter to the topic of professional renewal to illustrate the contrast between the Inside-out approach—practitioner-as-expert and theorist-as-practitioner—with the Outside-in approach—theorist-as-expert and practitioner-as-consumer.

# Mutual Adaptation in Staff Development: The RAND Study

In addition to investigating successful and unsuccessful implementation efforts, the RAND study also reviewed factors associated with success and failure in staff development (McLaughlin & Marsh, 1978). A summary of the five factors associated with successful staff development initiatives follows. [Heads added by this author.]

   I. *Teacher-as-Expert:*
   First, the study suggests that in terms of knowledge about the practice of teaching, teachers often represent the best clinical expertise available. (p. 87)

   II. *Local Adaptation:*
   Second, the RAND study describes the process by which an innovation comes to be used as adaptive. ... In a sense, teachers and administrative staff need to "reinvent the wheel" each time the innovation is brought into the school setting. Reinventing the wheel helps the teachers and administrative staff understand and adapt the innovation to local needs. (p. 87)

   III. *Long-Term, Non-Linear:*
   A third and related assumption communicated by the RAND study is that professional learning is a long-term, non-linear process. In the study, innovation sometimes took one or several years to achieve implementation. (p. 88)

   IV. *Administrator Involvement, Growth-Oriented:*
   A fourth assumption concerns viewing staff development as part of the program building process in school [which] also helped to shift staff development from a deficit model where teachers are seen as needing in-service training because they lack professional skills. ... Teachers were not the only group involved in project-skill development activities. Such an approach helped to spread and lessen the psychological risks of change. (pp. 88–89)

   V. *Organizational Support:*
   A fifth assumption concerns the importance of seeing staff development in the context of the school as an organizer. Within the most successful project, the project was not a "project" at all, but an integral part of an on-going problem-solving and improvement process within the school. In a sense, good staff development never ends. It is a continuous characteristic of the school site. (p. 90)

Like the RAND results on implementation, these RAND results on staff development were based on a great deal of evidence but, also like the strategies that worked in implementation, these principles of effective staff development have been largely ignored. In the following section, I describe a few examples of how these five principles can be used when working with practitioners in professional renewal activities. My purpose is to show my theorist/researcher colleagues that when they shed their theorist-as-expert role, they assume the new and even more challenging role of facilitating reciprocal relationships with practitioners. They become resources for each other—and this facilitation requires expertise.

# How I Apply the RAND Principles to Staff Development

When I receive an inquiry from a school or a district about the possibility of my working with the staff to develop some professional renewal activities, the five principles of McLaughlin and Marsh provide a mental checklist for me: (1) teacher-as-expert, (2) local adaptation, (3) long-term professional learning, (4) growth-oriented learning, and (5) organizational and administrative support.

1. Is the teacher acknowledged as the source of expertise?
2. Do teachers have responsibility for local adaptation?
3. Is their professional renewal long term?
4. Is the purpose of professional renewal to promote teacher/administrator growth rather than to correct deficits?
5. Is staff development visibly supported by the administration through its actions?

Most of the requests I receive are for a one-shot workshop, so my mental questions remain unanswered. I regard these five principles as goals to be attained during a negotiation phase that establishes the collaborative arrangements. In the past few years my initial work with teachers has always been a version of the workshop *Identifying Your Own Learning Style,* described in Chapter 3.

In Ontario, where I do most of my work, the Ministry of Education mandates a fixed number of professional development (PD) days in which the public schools are closed and the teachers engage in professional development activities. These activities frequently include district-wide PD Days, which feature a keynote speaker followed by workshops. I usually accept such invitations even though the initial activity meets none of the five principles because participating provides an opening to negotiate with the school or board on working toward some of the necessary steps for effective staff development in return for my work with the teachers.

For example, on receiving an invitation from a nearby school board a few years ago to "do something on learning style" with 500 elementary teachers on a PD Day, my response was to draft a letter of understanding describing our agreed-upon responsibilities. I asked the board to agree (1) to request that the director and all senior administrative officials participate in a half-day learning style workshop prior to the PD Day, (2) to arrange for 30 teachers or central staff personnel to volunteer for another half-day workshop and to work at follow-up sessions in the school, and (3) to provide a yet-to-be-determined amount of money, to be allocated by the teachers, for teacher follow-up (e.g., for materials, planning time, etc.). In turn, I agreed to conduct the two workshops prior to the workshop with 500 teachers and to assist with follow-up activities. Board officials generally agreed and the work proceeded in a collaborative fashion. Of course, it is not always possible to transform a one-shot PD Day into the first step in a more sustained professional renewal initiative, but I try to negotiate toward this goal as much as possible. As I write this segment, I realize that I am using these five principles as a blueprint to transform the initial Outside-in request into an Inside-out initiative.

Sometimes it is possible to transform a request for me to serve in the role of theorist-as-expert directly into the role of teacher-as-expert. I recently received a request from a committee of classroom teachers planning a three-session in-service program for other teachers who would be teaching summer school. Their initial request was for me to deliver a series of three lectures on learning style in the classroom. After a two-hour discussion we worked out a very different program in which I played a very different role. Based on the specific concerns voiced by teachers who had not taught summer school before, we developed a program to be presented by teachers with summer school experience. My role was that of moderator; I tried to integrate the various comments from the teacher panels and occasionally chimed in with a point from my own experience. The three-session program was well received and the spirit of teacher-as-expert was affirmed.

Sometimes failures are as important as successes in illustrating a point, and my batting average in following RAND principles is certainly not 1.000. I recently proposed a collaborative program of professional renewal for one board of education. When my proposal was accepted plans went forward, but *without* my proposed active involvement of the central administration (of which I had been assured in my letter of negotiation). My proposal was explicit in spelling out the necessity of administrative support and, in spite of the fact that the teachers on the planning committee were highly committed, the initiative failed primarily because of the lack of administrative support.

## Inside-Out or Outside-In in Staff Development

Although it may not always be possible to organize professional renewal activities on the basis of Inside-out approaches, it should be emphasized that there are many benefits resulting from such approaches.

### Promotes Professional Confidence

When practitioners are given the time and opportunity to identify their own theories, they are usually surprised and pleased to discover how much they know. This explication of their experienced knowledge affirms their adequacy and promotes their professional self-confidence.

### Facilitates Sharing Between Practitioners

The increase in the practitioners' individual feelings of confidence is greatly amplified when they share their own theories. By sharing theories they become aware of the expertise and know-how available from their colleagues and become potential resources for one another.

### Provides a Perspective From Which to Consider Structured Materials and Packages

Once practitioners have affirmed their professional confidence and have become aware that their practitioner colleagues are valuable resources, they can look at materials of the Outside-in variety (curriculum packages, formal theories, etc.) from their new perspective—that of an equal, a theorist with experienced knowledge.

Although I do not object to the use of Outside-in materials in a program, I sometimes disagree with *when* they are used and in *what form*. Practitioners who have affirmed their own ideas and ways of working are now free to reject them completely or to transform an entire package or part of it to suit their own theories and ways of working. This is what experienced teachers have always done, but the point is important in planning programs for professional renewal. First, if structured packages are used they should be introduced only after the practitioners have clearly identified their own theories and shared them with their colleagues. Inside-out must come before Outside-in. Second, if structured materials are used later in this program, they should be made available in a form that is easily *transformable* (i.e., a rough draft rather than a slick package, one that will permit practitioners to remove parts and adapt the package to their own purposes).

My major task is to help create a collaborative climate in which experienced practitioners can share their experienced knowledge or, more precisely, help to bring about the necessary conditions for the five RAND principles to be operative. What conditions are needed to have teachers regarded as experts? To bring about visible administrative support? Each of the RAND principles must be considered and encouraged.

Although effective staff development should be long-term, locally based, and growth-oriented, much of what is called professional development has been, is, and will continue to be accomplished in a one-shot, single-day format. If this option is non-negotiable, professional development need not be entirely a waste of time, and to this end I would make the following suggestions: (1) that opportunities for teachers to talk with each other informally at coffee breaks and lunch be maximized (the program should be planned around the breaks, not the other way around); (2) that presentations be made by other teachers, if possible; (3) that presentations by outsiders be light and humorous, providing a chance to relax and enjoy; and (4) that rather than trying to pack all the content into presentations, it should be provided as take-home material with clear instructions for possible follow-up or further questions.

## Overcoming Resistance in Changing the Image of Practice-Theory Relations

I would like to conclude this chapter on an upbeat note, but it would not ring true unless the discord of resistance from those who hold to the one-way Theory → Practice image is acknowledged. I am indebted to Richard deCharms for pointing out that the unilateral Theory → Practice image is a specific version of the one-way Mind → Body image, and even my Little Optimist would not try to solve the Mind-Body problem in a concluding paragraph.

Over the past ten years I have presented to dozens of groups of both practitioners and theorists/researchers my ideas on reversing the image to Practice → Theory in order to establish more reciprocal relations. The responses of the two groups has been striking. When I make these proposals to an audience of practitioners, such as experienced classroom teachers, their usual response is to smile, look at each other knowingly, and wonder if I am serious. When they realize that I am, valuable discussion results. When I make these proposals to an audience of theorists, their reactions remind me of the catalog of resolutions proposed by Fritz Heider for describing how people respond to negative and unpleasant communications. They think I am kidding (denial), they misunderstand what I am saying (distortion), or they think I am going soft in the head (devaluation of source). Perhaps the challenge of changing the Practice ↔ Theory image is better approached with a model of conflict resolution than with one of interpersonal communication. In any case, my suggestions here are iden-

## Practice-Theory Relations

tical to those I made to theorists at the conclusion of Chapter 6: "Try it, you may like it."

I conclude this chapter with a quote from Little's (1984) paper, "Seductive Images and Organizational Realities in Professional Development."

> Studies of effective professional development programs have proliferated in recent years, spawning a host of compelling images: collaboration, cooperation, partnership, mutual adaptation or accomplishment, collegiality, and interactive development among them. Such images are seductive, creating a vision of professional work and professional relations at once intellectually stimulating, educationally rigorous, and professionally rewarding. On closer examination, however, conditions that are powerful enough to introduce new ideas and practices in classrooms and to sustain "collegial" relations among teachers require a degree of organization, energy, skill, and endurance often underestimated in summary reports. A closer look reveals the challenge of organization and leadership, and uncovers the strains that accompany (and perhaps yield) the triumphs. (Little, 1984, p. 84)

# 8

# Beginning with Ourselves in Interpersonal Relations

> When you consider that each of us engages in dozens of interpersonal transactions every day—formally in our teaching, counseling, and supervision as well as informally with our colleagues, friends, and relatives—it is surprising that there are so few attempts to characterize such events. There are some interpersonal models, Transaction Analysis being perhaps the most familiar, but when compared to the universality of interpersonal experience, the number of models is very small. Why this disparity? (Abbey, Hunt, & Weiser, 1985, p. 477)

To study interpersonal transactions requires attention to persons-in-relation, yet mainstream psychology focuses only on encapsulated individuals who, by definition, do not interact (cf. Sarason, 1981). Another reason for this disparity is that mainstream psychology evaluates all theories according to their logic, consistency, and research support—criteria that are less relevant for interpersonal theories than for the way in which they match our experience in interpersonal affairs. Since everyone has a wealth of experienced knowledge about interpersonal transactions, the criterion for such theoretical models should be the degree to which they agree with our own experience and implicit theories.

This chapter features our "Variations on a Theme by Kolb" (Abbey et al., 1985), which uses Kolb's experiential learning cycle (1984) to develop a model of interpersonal transactions or persons-in-relation. Given my strong emphasis on Inside-out, it may seem surprising that in this final chapter I offer an Outside-in model for your consideration. I invite you to approach this chapter as an exercise in using your own theories as a basis for considering the value of other theories (from Inside-out to Outside-in); consequently, you need to keep your own implicit theories in mind as you read it. After reading these explicit theories, you may want to transform them or translate some of their terms into your own theories. The major purpose of this chapter is to bring our theories to an interpersonal level to show how they can guide our actions in both professional and personal affairs.

I begin by briefly reviewing the tentative framework that I developed on the Mutual Adaptation Project for viewing interpersonal transactions. The second section describes our "Variation on a Theme by Kolb," the primary model for this chapter. Kolb's model is also used to develop a practical guide for applying the cycle to personal and professional concerns, which I call C-RE-A-T-E. This chapter concludes by noting that in giving primacy to direct experience, Kolb's experiential learning cycle provides a conceptual basis for beginning with ourselves.

# A Mutual Adaptation View of Interpersonal Relations

In Chapter 7, I described how our Mutual Adaptation Project was carried out by collaborating with teachers to initiate a climate of mutual adaptation in classrooms. The project characterized classroom transactions between student and student and between student and teacher as well as our transactions in collaboration, between teacher-researcher. These concrete and specific transactions served as the basis for developing a tentative framework to characterize persons-in-relation—not only teacher-student and researcher-teacher, but also other interpersonal transactions (e.g., parent-child and husband-wife).

The initial framework grew out of an attempt to specify the processes of "reading" and "flexing" in greater detail and was initially stated for one person rather than for between persons, as shown in Figure 8–1 (Hunt, 1976b).

# Figure 8-1

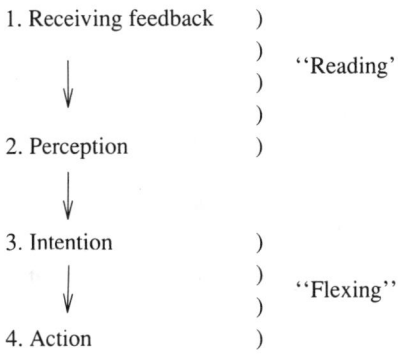

I remind you to activate your implicit theories, your past experience (personal and professional), and your common sense in considering this model.

These four components were then put into a transactional pattern (Hunt, 1982b) that consisted of a continuous transactional cycle between the two participants (e.g., teacher and student), as shown in Figure 8-2.

# Figure 8-2

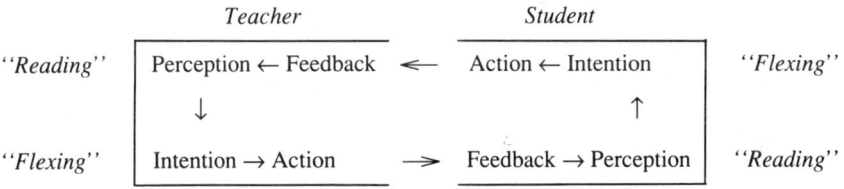

Figure 8-2 shows a framework within which all interpersonal transactions can be characterized, but for our purposes the example is that of teacher and student. This is not intended to imply that both parties are always aware of perception and intention; in fact, most interpersonal transactions take place in a split-second cycle, of the kind shown in Figure 8-3, with no awareness of perception or intention.

### Figure 8-3

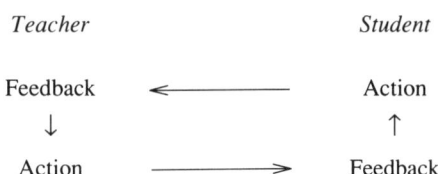

When teachers are given time to reflect on their actions, as in *How To Be Your Own Best Theorist,* they may bring out their implicit theories, as Figure 8-4 shows.

### Figure 8-4

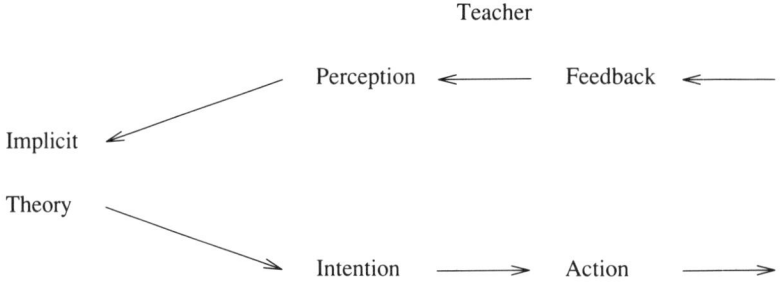

One way to illustrate the terms I use in this sequence is to consider how they would apply to the phrases in *How To Be Your Own Best Theorist* in Chapter 4. This is illustrated in Table 8-1.

### Table 8-1

**How To Be Your Own Best Theorist**

| Component | Description | Phases in Mutual Adaptation Framework |
|---|---|---|
| Person | Student characteristic | Perception |
| Behavior | Goal | Intention |
| Environment | Teaching approach | Action |
| Implicit theory | Matching model | Implicit theory |

Interpersonal Relations    149

Putting your implicit theory into action to test it would provide feedback. I have merely sketched my tentative framework but have done so primarily to show you its similarity to Kolb's cycle and to show why I have found playing variations on this cycle so helpful.

# Variations on a Theme by Kolb

The following is excerpted from "Variations on a Theme by Kolb"(Abbey et al., 1985).

> We ask you to use your personal criteria in evaluating the model we present. Does it fit with your experience? Does it feel right? Does it shed new light on your experience? As George Kelly would have said, try it on for size. We do not intend that you entirely abandon conventional criteria such as logical consistency and experimental evidence, only that you suspend judgment on them initially while you apply personal criteria. (Abbey et al., 1985, p. 478)

## The Theme from Kolb:
## An Experiential Learning Cycle

[Kolb's theory of experiential learning (Kolb, 1975, 1984) is based on a four-phase cycle of experiential learning which he described as follows (italics ours):]

> The underlying insight of experiential learning is deceptively simple, namely that learning, change and growth are best facilitated by an integrated process that begins with (1) here-and-now *experience* followed by (2) collection of data and *observation* about experience. The data are then (3) *analyzed* and the conclusions of the analysis are fed back to the actors in the experience for their use in the (4) modification of the *behavior* and choices of new experiences. Learning is thus conceived as a four-stage cycle as shown in [Figure 8-5]. ... Immediate *concrete experience* is the basis for observation and reflection. These observations are assimilated into a "theory" from which new implications for *action* can be deduced. (Kolb, 1975, pp. 33-34)

## Figure 8-5
## Kolb's Experiential Learning Cycle

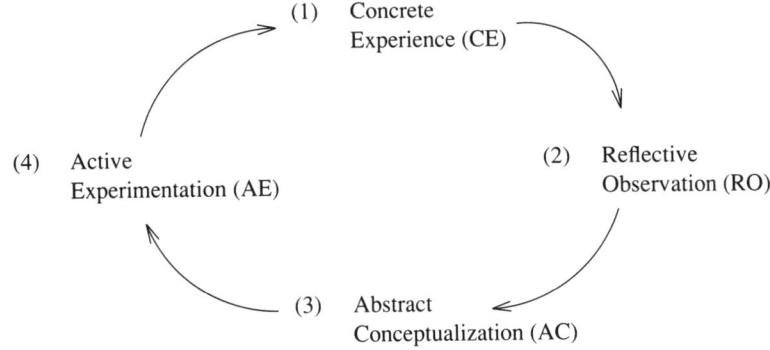

*Source:* adapted from Kolb, 1975

[Note that the four modes in the Kolb cycle can be inserted into the earlier transactional model, as shown in Figure 8-6.]

## Figure 8-6

```
        Person 1                           Person 2

"Flexing"   AC → AE     ─────────▶   CE → RO     "Reading"
              ↑                         ↓
"Reading"   RO ← CE     ◀─────────   AE ← AC     "Flexing"
```

# Variation I: Identifying and Activating Modes of Experience

In this section we elaborate the phases as distinguishable *modes of experience* by describing how you can identify them in yourself and how you can recognize and attempt to *activate* them in others. Segmenting the whole of the experiential cycle into its component parts runs the risk of what has been called paralysis-by-analysis—unless we bear in mind that the purpose of identifying the parts is to give more meaning to the whole. As you try to identify the distinct modes, think of it as distinguishing between speaking and listening when engaging in the continuous flow of conversation. Identifying the distinct modes of experience has the same intention as identifying the mode of listening in order to improve it.

## Identifying Modes of Experience

We begin by inviting you to identify each mode by experiencing it. If you accept our invitation to try these modes for yourself, you should plan to spend a few minutes with the following four points rather than the few seconds required to read them.

1. *Identifying Feeling Mode:* By its definition, an experiential cycle begins with concrete experience and feelings. Pay attention to your feelings at this moment. Try to be aware of your immediate emotional experience. Stop reading in a moment, look up, and focus on your feelings. Don't move and don't be concerned about putting words on your feelings; let them appear. Now try it. . . . Remember you are attempting to experience your feelings as distinctly and vividly as possible. Continue this identifying of the experience of your immediate feelings as long as necessary, noting how easy or difficult it seems.
2. *Identifying Reflecting Mode:* Now sit back and review what has been happening in the last few moments. In a moment, stop reading and try to recapture exactly what has happened as you engaged in this identification exercise. Become detached so that you can observe and consider what has been going on. Think of yourself as an observer looking at and listening in on your own direct experience. Don't worry about making meaning as you recapture what happened, just try to replay it as clearly and vividly as possible. Consider how easy or difficult this was for you.
3. *Identifying Conceptualizing Mode:* Now it is time to try to make sense of what has been going on. While reviewing what has happened, try to give some meaning to what you have been experiencing and observing. Try to develop a concept which will link together what has happened. Pay attention to the relation between the various experiences, and try to create a basis for understanding what went on. Note how easy or difficult this seemed.
4. *Identifying Action Mode:* Now that you have given meaning to what you have experienced, take some action on the basis of your conceptual understanding. Your action may be very active, e.g., to go and tell someone else about what you have just experienced, or less active, e.g., writing down a plan or deciding to reread the last three sections of this paper. Be aware of the action as distinct from the thinking. Also be aware as you act that you will experience feelings associated with the action which will activate the cycle again. Note how easy or difficult it is for you to take action.

At this point we hope that you have developed an intuitive feel for the distinctive characteristics of each of the four modes. Also, as you look back at your attempt to experience each mode, consider which one was easiest and which one seemed most difficult, as this will give an indication of which modes are most highly developed and which are undeveloped in your experience. We discuss these patterns in Variation II below, but first we consider briefly how a counselor might help a client activate or focus on each mode.

## Activating Modes of Experience in Counseling

Having become aware of each mode in your own experience, you may now consider how you might help a client to activate a specific mode. In this section we describe what are usually considered counseling "moves," strategies, or interventions in terms of their aim to activate one of these specific modes in the client. Such activation may be aimed at continuing the flow, e.g., going from RO to AC, or it may be to help the client return to a mode, e.g., back to CE. The following dialogues show how a counselor might respond to a client statement, giving examples for activating each specific mode:

*Client:* Yes, it is going a little bit too long, what do I do about it?

Counselor comments to activate:

*CE:* What is the feeling like, how would you describe it?
Try to experience that feeling now.

*RO:* Is it like any other feelings you have?
What thoughts usually follow these feelings?

*AC:* What do you make of all this?
Why do you think it keeps going so long?

*AE:* What have you tried?
Is there anything that worked for you before?

\* \* \*

*Client:* I can really feel, you know, getting to a sort of slanted sad direction.

Counselor comments to activate:

*CE:* Tell me more about that feeling.
Slanted and sad.

*RO:* What direction will it take?
Slanted?

*AC:* What do you make of it?
Why do you think it takes this direction?

*AE:* Then what do you do?
Have you tried anything to prevent its happening?

## Variation II: Characterizing Persons in Terms of Modes of Experience

In attempting to identify each mode in yourself in the exercises just described, you probably noticed that some modes were more easily activated and identified than others, e.g., you may have found it very easy to activate conceptualizing, but more difficult to activate your feeling mode. In this section we use this differential accessibility of the four modes to derive patterns which characterize persons in terms of those modes which are highly developed in terms of reflecting (RO), conceptualizing (AC), and acting (AE), but undeveloped in feeling (CE).

Before describing these specific patterns, we note two differences between our variation and that of Kolb. First, rather than the paper-and-pencil measures used by Kolb—Learning Style Inventory (LSI) (Kolb, 1976) and Adaptive Style Inventory (ASI) (Kolb, 1984, pp. 213–217; Kolb, Wolfe, et al., 1981)—we propose to assess these patterns "in the moment" (Hunt, 1982a) through a person's words and actions. We later show how a counselor might assess or "read" a client's patterns from what a client says and does in the counseling situation. Second, in contrast to the LSI, which classifies persons into one of the four quadrants in Figure 8–5 (e.g., scores in the upper right quadrant CE-RO are known as "convergers"), we characterize persons in terms of how well developed they are in each of the four modes. Our scheme of characterizing individual variation is much more similar to Kolb's more recent ASI (Kolb, 1984) than to the earlier LSI.

In describing the patterns we use the four directions of the compass to designate the four modes: North = CE; East = RO; South = AC; and West = AE. These compass points serve to describe patterns of three-mode, two-mode, and one-mode functions. For example, a Northerner pattern refers to a three-mode pattern in the "Northern hemisphere" of the cycle, e.g. CE → RO → AE, while Northeastern refers to a two-mode pattern of CE → RO → CE; single-mode patterns are called, for example, North only, CE. All of these patterns are viewed as relatively imbalanced compared to the ideal, in which all four modes would be equally and fully developed in a balanced pattern. We use the terms well developed and undeveloped to describe the differential accessibility of the modes in a specific pattern to convey the idea that an undeveloped mode, though limiting, can become the object of development. We do not view them as strengths and weaknesses, or strong modes and deficits, because the terms deficit and weakness imply that the modes will remain weak, an implication which is completely against the spirit of this model.

### Three-Mode Patterns

In each of these patterns, three modes are well developed and one undeveloped; we represent these modes by a half-circle to depict diagrammatically the nature of the three-part cycle.

## Figure 8-7
## Three-Mode Patterns: Underdevelopment of One Mode of Experience

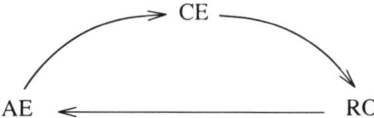

AC

The "Northerner": Underdevelopment of
Abstract Conceptualization (AC)

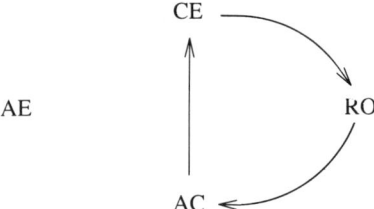

The "Easterner": Underdevelopment of
Active Experimentation (AE)

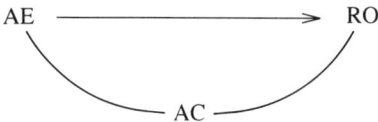

The "Southerner": Underdevelopment of
Concrete Experience (CE)

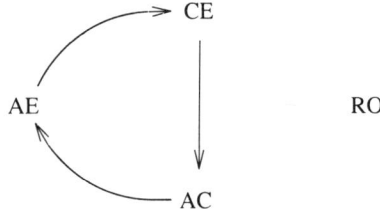

The "Westerner": Underdevelopment of
Reflective Observation (RO)

# Interpersonal Relations

1. *Northerner:* This person has difficulty in conceptualizing or making meaning of experience; consequently, the cycle runs from feelings to reflection (which remains unconsolidated) to action. The consequence of this Northerly pattern is that the flow is discontinuous and the actions are poorly organized since they are not informed by the foundation of AC meaning. By developing the AC mode, the Northerly pattern becomes more balanced, the AE more of a piece.
2. *Easterner:* Persons with an Easterly pattern have trouble putting plans into action (AE). Consequently, they spend much time "buried in thought." Because the AE mode is short-circuited, their thoughts (AC) are about their feelings (CE) rather than about their direct actions; this imbalanced cycle lacks the rejuvenation provided by actions. With the development of AE, then the other modes would be fully functioning, and directed to informing actions.
3. *Southerner:* Persons with a Southerly pattern are "not in touch with their feelings." They reflect on the mechanics of their actions (AE) without benefit of emotional feedback. The reflection may lead to reformulation of concepts (AC), but the revision is mechanical and sterile. If the CE mode were to be developed, then the cycle would recover the vitality provided by the feeling mode, and the other three modes become more fluid and alive.
4. *Westerner:* In this pattern, the Westerner goes directly from feeling to conceptualizing without sorting out the concrete experience. Consequently, the initial conceptual framework is likely to be unclear, with little possibility to correct it through reflection. With the development of RO, the Westerner orientation becomes balanced through the clarification of feelings through the RO mode (Abbey et al., 1985, pp. 478–487).

Because our article was written for counselors who work with poorly adjusted persons, it went on to describe two-mode and single-mode patterns that might be considered non-adaptive (i.e., those persons were "stuck," many of them in need of some form of therapy). We assumed that most professionals—practitioners, consultants, theorists, and researchers—would have three fairly well-developed modes and one relatively undeveloped one. The developed modes are not always used but they are available.

Although counselor-client transactions were described in transcripts (Abbey et al., 1985, pp. 489–499), we did not explicitly take the Kolb cycle from its original experiential form to an interpersonal level. I sketch briefly how the cycle might be applied to interpersonal transactions, acknowledging that such an account is bound to be incomplete. Figure 8–8 shows how the Kolb cycle might be applied to an interpersonal sequence (e.g., two people in conversation). It is based on the components in the mutual adaptation sequence, which are placed in parentheses.

## Figure 8-8

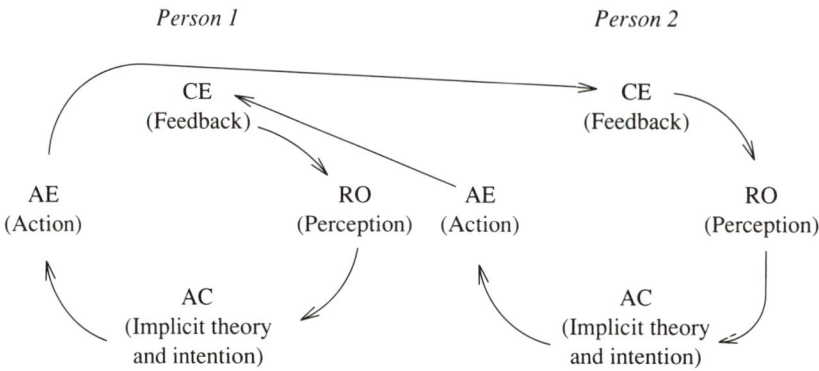

Figure 8-8 is enormously compressed and, like the previous cycles, is intended as an ideal model and not meant to imply that each phase will always occur. This figure poses certain questions: Is the AC mode the same as the intention phase? Does a person in conversation go through all four modes? Acknowledging the tentative nature of this view, I ask that you "try it on for size" in relation to your own implicit theories and see how it may help you take action in some of your professional and personal concerns.

Although it complicates the model, I intentionally express this sequence using two different sets of concepts: (1) Kolb (CE → RO → AC → AE) and (2) Hunt (Feedback → Perception → Implicit Theory → Intention → Action) because I hope to show how a view can be expressed in two different "languages" that seem to provide equivalent translations of the interpersonal process.

Sketchy as it is, Figure 8-8 is valuable for three reasons. First, Kolb's experiential cycle fits in very well with my experience and beliefs and enhances my understanding. Second, this view of interpersonal transactions is the only one I have found that provides both a characterization of the two participants in terms of each one's orientation (e.g., a Southerner) and an account of their specific interpersonal transactions through the same framework. There are numerous learning style models for characterizing persons, but this is the only one in my experience in which the framework for classification also provides a framework for the process of analyzing specific interpersonal communication (cf. Abbey et al., 1985, pp. 489-499, for analyses of counseling transcripts). For example, a supervisor who is a Northerner will likely find it difficult (or will altogether neglect) to help the trainee find concepts (AC) or give meaning to the case being discussed. This point is complex but important and is related to the third reason for the value of this model—these modes (e.g., CE) or components

# Interpersonal Relations 157

(e.g., receiving feedback) may be looked upon as complex skills that can be developed either in professional training or in personal development (Hunt, 1982b).

Before continuing, stop for a moment and reflect on how well the cycle fits your own implicit theories and experience, and consider how well the interpersonal sequence fits your views of and experience in human affairs. What a little RO can do for you!

## Applying the Cycle: C-RE-A-T-E

I played still another variation on the Kolb theme by transforming his cycle into a C-RE-A-T-E cycle (Figure 8–9), which provides practitioners with a guide to apply their implicit theories to their professional concerns. The five steps in the C-RE-A-T-E cycle are:

1. *C*oncern: State your concern (e.g., perhaps you are having difficulty communicating with one of your students or clients).
2. *RE*flect: Summarize your implicit theories in the form of your intentions, matching models, and metaphors (as in the examples in Chapter 5).
3. *A*nalyze: Apply your implicit theories and experienced knowledge to your concern to develop an action plan.
4. *T*ry out: Try your plan in action.
5. *E*xperience: Note the feedback from your action, evaluate it, and go through the cycle again.

**Figure 8–9**

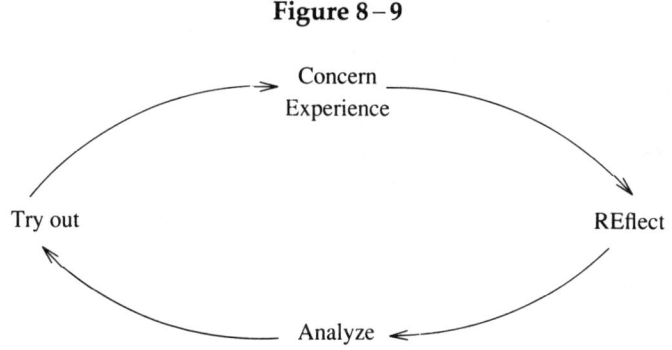

The C-RE-A-T-E cycle both illustrates the Kolb cycle and provides a basis for practitioners to apply their implicit theories to their concerns. I have recently discovered that the C-RE-A-T-E cycle becomes even more valuable when used in groups; it provides a guide for practitioners to share their experienced knowledge and to focus their collective wisdom on the concern of one member of the group. Let me illustrate with an example of an account taken from a group of five counselors applying the C-RE-A-T-E cycle in my learning styles class:

1. *C*oncern: We focused on the concern of one of the counselors in our group: a 15-year-old girl in the tenth grade who was on the verge of being kicked out of school for her aggressive behavior. She was bright and doing well academically but associated with a tough crowd who got into serious physical fights.
2. *RE*flect: The counselor's metaphor was that of a pilgrim monk helping other pilgrims on the trip of life: "How we go is more important than getting there." With one exception, the other members of the group used similar metaphors.

    After some discussion, the counselor felt that a different kind of metaphor was required, one that had not been considered: "I picture myself as the magician who keeps all the plates spinning on the long rods and has to keep running back and forth to keep the plates going and prevent them from falling and breaking." [Mary Shawcross' metaphor discussed in Chapter 4.]

    This metaphor captured the necessity of taking immediate action to help the client. Since expulsion from school was an imminent threat, "guiding" her slowly "along the path of life" was an inappropriate luxury. It was much more appropriate to visualize how "all the plates had to be kept spinning in the air—or they would fall and break."
3. *A*nalyze: We decided that the client was very much a "doer," one who learned through *active experimentation.* Therefore, the client needed very specific action-oriented suggestions. The counselor had already approached her in this mode, giving her a concrete suggestion that, if provoked, she should put her arms by her side, not say or do anything, and come directly to the counselor's office. The counselor's learning style was primarily that of a "Northerner," although she had access to the AC mode. The client did very little reflecting on feelings, which was the counselor's preferred style. With the spinning plates as the metaphor, the following plan of action was developed, which proved successful.

    - To check in with the client the next day at school rather than wait several days. One in the group whose strongest modality was *active*

# Interpersonal Relations

*experimentation* made this suggestion, which fit in aptly with the spinning plate metaphor. The plan was also to see her more frequently.
- To capitalize on her action orientation and leadership skills by encouraging her to help others. This was accomplished by having her go for an interview with a co-op program that would require her to help out with children in an after-school drop-in program. She liked the idea and has already picked out a student she feels she can help; he's a "fighter," like herself.

This action plan continued in more detail and proved very successful in the *Try* out phase. This case illustrates not only how C-RE-A-T-E can serve as a general guide for practitioners to pool their experienced knowledge but also how they can use the language of metaphor to share views. Like stinger reversal, changing to a different metaphor provides a fresh, and potentially valuable, change in perspective.

This initial experience in using the C-RE-A-T-E cycle in a group situation supports my hunch that metaphors may give practitioners a heretofore hidden language, one that will unlock their experienced knowledge and open the door for them to become resources to one another. I initially described this group process as "structured brainstorming," which is partly true, but it should involve more than just the brain. As one participant described the process of metaphor exchange: "We *lived* our metaphors, acting them out in role playing." In this case, the C-RE-A-T-E cycle enabled the practitioners to communicate through the language of action.

The C-RE-A-T-E cycle is certainly not completely new. Counselors will see its similarity to many counseling models that prescribe beginning with the client's concern, reflecting, etc., while teachers may see its similarity to various models of problem solving and inquiry that state the problem, consider alternatives, and so on. Nonetheless, its initial applications show that even in one-day sessions practitioners find it relevant and energizing. It may also be applied to nonprofessional concerns, as one student-colleague observed:

> I have shared the CREATE cycle with family members, and even if one leaves out the technical terms, the cycle is still practical and effective. If one applies the CREATE cycle, then one helps to *create* a new relationship through the art of *creative* response. If one lives out the CREATE cycle, then one is *re-created* in the process.

The C-RE-A-T-E cycle is most effective when all participants have brought out their implicit theories and experienced knowledge, and have summarized their implicit theories for use in the *RE*flect phase. That practitioners summarize this information in a succinct, communicable form is a more important issue than it seems. I have experimented with asking colleagues to summarize their implicit theories on a single sheet by completing the following statements: (1) "My learning style ..."; (2) "My undeveloped mode ..."; (3) "The most important thing in my work is ..."; (4) "My metaphor of teaching-learning is ..."; (5) "My metaphor of matching is ..."; and (6) "My matching model is. ..."

Most of the exchange of ideas so far has been through metaphor exchange, but matching models ("If ... then ..." statements) and other statements may also be valuable resources. Developing the most appropriate ways to elicit those summaries in communicable form exemplifies what I define as the new role of psychologists—to facilitate communication between people, in this case, practitioners. The more experienced knowledge available as resource, the better the C-RE-A-T-E cycle works, but I have also experimented with using it when practitioners have only their metaphors, and even this limited use has shown promise.

# In the Beginning There Was Direct Experience

I conclude with a short discussion of the "two faces of concreteness" because distinguishing between them so clearly illustrates my shift from Outside-in to Inside-out and provides a conceptual legitimacy for beginning with ourselves. The two faces, or meanings, are (1) concreteness-as-inferior-thinking (i.e., as opposed to abstract or formal operational thinking) and (2) concreteness-as-direct-experience (i.e., the here-and-now immediacy of the present). Although these are very different meanings, they have not always been distinguished. Indeed, I want to show that in some cases their meanings are so blurred that, although it may not be expressed explicitly, concreteness-as-direct-experience takes on an inferior meaning, as is attributed to concreteness-as-inferior-thinking.

Concreteness-as-inferior-thinking is exemplified by Conceptual Systems Theory (Harvey et al., 1961), in which it is contrasted with the superior form of abstract thinking; Piaget's theory of formal operations, in which concrete thinking is a lower developmental stage, preceding that of formal operational thinking; and the similarities sub-test of the Wechsler-Bellevue Intelligence Test, in which answering a question like "How are a fork and spoon alike?" by responding with "utensils" is considered abstract, and therefore assigned a higher score than "You eat with both."

## Interpersonal Relations 161

Given my present emphasis on the primacy of concrete experience, it seems ironic that when Kolb originally (1971) proposed the concrete-abstract dimension, he cited Conceptual Systems Theory (Harvey et al., 1961) as a primary reference for legitimizing its importance. He acknowledged, but did not necessarily emphasize, the primacy of concrete experience. Here, and elsewhere, the two meanings became indistinguishably blurred, with the result that concreteness-as-direct-experience became inferior because it was not clearly distinguished from concreteness-as-inferior-thinking. One example of this confusion is seen in Kohlberg's conceptual scheme (1984) for moral thinking, which mainly involves the application of an abstract-concrete dimension to moral thinking. When Kohlberg assessed level of moral maturity by evaluating responses to moral dilemmas, the two meanings became indistinguishably blurred. For example, when respondents approached the hypothetical (abstract) dilemma by trying to put themselves into the experience directly and asking concrete questions about the situation, they were scored lower on the moral dimension (Gilligan, 1982). Because of this lack of distinction between the two meanings of concreteness, I prefer to use the term *direct experience*.

I believe that the single most important feature of the Kolb cycle is its emphasis on the primacy of direct experience (CE): "In the beginning there was direct experience." The primacy of direct experience has enabled me to take a new perspective on many old problems, not the least of which is that theorists usually believe that "In the beginning there was the blackboard" (the primacy of AC).

I hope that this summary of this curious chain of events clearly illustrates my progression to Inside-out. With concreteness no longer regarded as inferior to abstraction but, rather, placed at the beginning of the sequence of experiential learning, its primacy is redeemed. And so, after attempting to make my case for beginning with ourselves mainly on intuitive grounds, it is ironic to find that my case can also be made logically, based on this experiential cycle. It is indeed a curious state of affairs; Kolb used my earlier theory for one purpose, and now I am using his theory for quite another, in fact opposite, purpose. Who said that theorists can't learn from one another?

# Appendix
# How To Be
# Your Own Best Theorist*

## Workshop Purposes and Principles

The purpose of a workshop in identifying your own theories is (1) to enhance self-knowledge and (2) to facilitate communication. Since "Teachers are Psychologists, Too" (Hunt, 1976a) and "Theorists Are Persons, Too" (Hunt, 1978a), all participants, including the leader, are colleagues working together to identify and share their theories. To maximize feedback, all information is circulated so that each participant can see all theories. To respect individual privacy, information is anonymous, but participants are free to disclose their own theories if they choose. Workshop discussions are noncritical, with an emphasis on the personal validity of one's own theories and the information value of others' theories.

---

* The following is excerpted from Hunt, D.E. (1980a). How to be your own best theorist. *Theory into Practice, 19,* September, 287–293.

# A Workshop to Identify Your Implicit Theories

A workshop to identify implicit theories took place over five weekly three-hour sessions as the first part of an evening course I taught at OISE [Ontario Institute for Studies in Education] in the fall of 1979. The participants were 21 graduate students, primarily part-time master's level, who ranged widely in their practice from pre-school teachers to psychotherapists.

## Different Settings and Groups

When a workshop is part of a credit course taught by a professor at a university, the setting and role relations are obstacles to the development of an open, reciprocal workshop climate. For example, practitioner-students enter OISE expecting we will deliver our explicit theories to them; after all, we are the Department of Educational Theory at the University of Toronto. One way to decrease the leader-professor's Expert role and to increase the legitimacy of the practitioner-students' implicit, practical theories is to conduct the workshop course in the participants' school. (I recently taught a credit course at a local junior high school.) Another way to further decrease the role of the leader as Expert or Evaluator is for another teacher to teach a non-credit workshop, i.e., the teacher center model. However, it seems likely that many teachers will continue to seek professional development in colleges and universities, and this example focuses on workshops in that setting.

When the participants come from the same school, their common experience will serve as a basis for them to share ideas. A team of teachers may even share the same students. When participants come from very diverse settings, they begin with little in common, but often discover unexpectedly similar concerns, e.g., a teacher and a counselor became aware of working in similar ways with their students and clients.

Even in large groups, people get some idea of their implicit theories, and I often begin a formal address with a miniature version of this exercise to give members of the audience a personal base for considering my explicit theories. It may also pique their interest for later trying a longer version. On the other hand, one person alone can participate in most of the exercises and this may enhance self-knowledge, though of course it is less likely to facilitate communication.

## Introduction to Workshop

Because the workshop took place as part of a graduate course, I began by (1) describing the procedures and the workshop principles; (2) distinguishing our role relations in the workshop from those in a conventional graduate course; and (3) emphasizing that none of the workshop experience would be evaluated or used in determining grades. Appropriate chapters in our B-P-E book (Hunt & Sullivan, 1974) were assigned to illustrate the B-P-E way of thinking.

I now invite you to become an imaginary member of the workshop, and since it is described according to the seven steps in your miniature version, you can lend reality to the image by consulting your sheets whenever needed.

## Step 1:
## Describing Your Whole Concept of Your Work

[Instructions are to imagine you are writing for a colleague—someone with whom you are comfortable—to express what is most important in your work and how you go about it. Write about your work for 5 minutes.] Summarizing one's overall foundation helps later to see relations between parts which might otherwise seem disconnected. We need this whole to give meaning and coherence to the parts, and see how they fit together. In this workshop, participants retained their own summaries for later use, although these could be circulated anonymously to the group.

## Step 2:
## Selecting Parts of the Whole (B-P-E)

The three initials on your second sheet (P-B-E) are taken from Kurt Lewin's idea that Behavior depends on the interaction of the Person and the Environment, and adapted for education (Hunt & Sullivan, 1974) as the outcome (B) resulting from a student (P) experiencing an educational approach (E). The parts may be considered in different order for different purposes, e.g. E: $P \rightarrow B$ (from the teacher's perspective) or the P-B-E in the present instance. Don't be put off because its original form, $B = f(P,E)$, looks like a precise mathematical equation; Just think of B-P-E as a tool which may help to reduce the complexity of otherwise bewildering patterns in teaching and learning to understandable relations among the parts. B-P-E is not itself a theory, but a way of thinking about theories, yours and others', which I hope you will "try on for size."

# Steps 3 and 4:
# Identifying Your Concepts of Students (P)

This exercise comes from the work of the psychologist George Kelly (1955), who based his theories on the belief that every person is a psychologist, i.e., in our everyday dealings with others, we develop personal constructs, even though we are not always aware of them. To explicate one's personal constructs, Kelly devised the Role Concept Repertory (or Rep) Test, on which this exercise is based. I helped develop the original Rep Test (Hunt, 1951), yet it was a quarter-century later before I adapted it for teachers (Hunt, 1976a). If you find this education-specific Rep Test valuable, you may wish to try the more personal, non-school version in the original (Kelly, 1955, pp. 219–233). I have been using the terms "concept" (or "construct") and "theory" interchangeably, but I need now to note that Steps 4, 5 and 6 identify your concepts while Step 7 expresses the relations among these concepts in terms of your theory.

The Rep Test identifies only the content of your constructs, not their structure or openness to change, which require additional methods. Like the B-P-E way of thinking, the Rep Test is a guide, indeed a very specific guide, to construct identification. In taking the Rep Test, try to follow instructions as much as possible, bearing in mind that the purpose is to explicate ten of your constructs. Try not to get stuck in thinking of a student who meets a description (alter the description slightly) or get bogged down in sorting (just pick the two who are most alike). Come as close as you can to the instructions, but adapt them if necessary.

**Rep Test Instructions**

1. Using twelve 3" x 5" cards (or similar size pieces of paper), number from 1 to 12 in the upper right hand corner.

2. Using the following descriptions, write the names of students you know or have known. If you have not taught, write the name of a person you know who fits the description. Select 12 different persons so that you have 12 different names on the cards. (No one else will see the names; they are only for your use.) [Other professionals adapt the role titles, e.g., counselors identify clients. The role titles are only guides for identifying those persons with whom you work.]

    1. The first male student whose name comes to mind.
    2. A female student you found hard to understand.
    3. A male student you would like to help.
    4. The first female student who comes to mind.
    5. A male student you would like to know better.
    6. A female student you would like to help.
    7. A male student whom you liked.
    8. A female student whom you liked.

## How To Be Your Own Best Theorist

    9. A male student whom you don't like.
   10. A female student whom you don't like.
   11. A male student you found hard to understand.
   12. A female student you would like to know better.

3. Next, select cards No. 1, No. 4, and No. 8, and place them before you. After asking yourself: "Which two of these three are alike in some important way and different from the third?" select those two and put them together. Next, ask yourself: "How are they alike?" describing this similarity in your own words by a word or phrase. Using the attached sheet, circle the two persons alike and write your word or phrase describing how you see them as being alike. Continue this procedure for the following nine triads (try to write ten different descriptions): (2) 2–5–9; (3) 3–7–10; (4) 4–6–11; (5) 1–5–12; (6) 2–6–9; (7) 3–4–10; (8) 5–6–11; (9) 7–8–9; (10) 10–11–12.

Participants completed the Rep Test during the week, and left their recording sheets to be duplicated.

### Feedback and Discussion

At the next session, feedback sheets containing all participants' lists of student concepts (identified only by code letter) were distributed. Discussion began with reaction to the Rep Test: "I had trouble thinking of a student I don't like," "I was surprised at some of my groupings." When asked if their lists seemed personally valid, participants often expressed concern that their constructs seemed limited to these particular students and the specific circumstances in which they were taught. We then considered the sources of our constructs—the students, the context, and ourselves—to determine how well they represented our true implict concepts.

Next, a manual for scoring person concepts was distributed. This manual is based largely on the student concepts expressed by several hundred teachers earlier, and is intended only for this purpose. It consists of 18 categories: (1) sociability; (2) ability; (3) motivation; (4) responsibility; (5) honesty; (6) independence; (7) participation; (8) flexibility; (9) cooperation; (10) dominance; (11) creativity; (12) diligence; (13) sensitivity; (14) self-concept; (15) satisfaction; (16) maturity; (17) appearance; and (18) unscorable. Concepts were placed into categories, and then categories tallied for the whole group as well as for specific groups of participants—elementary teachers, secondary teachers, postsecondary teachers, counselors, consultants, etc.—so that the categories most often used by different practitioner groups could be considered. In addition to the manual categories, participants were also concerned about their use of positive or negative concepts.

### Comparison with Psychologists' Concepts of Persons

This exercise provides an intuitive experience for participants to consider topics such as individual differences or personality. They were interested that among all the person concepts on their feedback sheets were almost all of the formal concepts which psychologists have used to describe individual personality differences. Identifying their own concepts also gave participants a legitimate, personal base to view psychologists' formal theories, e.g., they commented that Skinner has no conception of a person in his theory. I used their concepts to illustrate "accessibility channels" and the developmental-contemporaneous distinction (Hunt & Sullivan, 1974, Chapter 2), which otherwise may be remote from practice.

### Other Possibilities

An additional approach is to ask participants, before they begin the Rep Test, simply to list ten of their ways of describing their students, and then compare this list of espoused-concepts with the Rep Test list which is closer to concepts-in-use (cf. Argyris & Schon, 1974, for espoused theory vs. theory-in-use). Espoused lists usually contained more socially desirable concepts, e.g., honesty, while the Rep Test lists were closer to practice, e.g., dominance, participation. Participants interested in assessing just how open to change their concepts are may use a forced-sorting" variation on Step 4 by considering two of the students in a triad not originally grouped together and attempting to "force" concepts about this pair of previously dissimilar students.

## Step 5:
## Identifying Your Concepts of Objectives

[See miniature exercise instructions in Chapter 4.] Consider the two persons circled in 1−4−8, and answer the question "How are these two alike in terms of my goals for them?" Record this goal and continue with the other nine pairs.

### Feedback and Discussion

These were similar to the feedback and discussion for P with the addition of comments on PB relations, since the order of participants on these feedback sheets was the same as for feedback sheets for P. Next, a manual for coding student behaviors was distributed, and participants coded their 10 constructs according to the 14 categories: (1) acquired knowledge or skill; (2) motivation; (3) interpersonal relations; (4) social-emotional development; (5) adjustment behavior; (6) self-concept; (7) cooperation; (8) responsibility; (9) independence; (10) work habits; (11) satisfaction; (12) physical health; (13) sources of influence; and (14) unscorable. This category system is very imprecise, especially in the variation in category specificity; e.g., "acquired knowledge or skill" is very general and might be subdivided while "physical health" is quite specific. However, the manual served its purpose, and we followed the same procedure of tallying category frequencies.

Some participants were surprised at the preponderance of cognitive or knowledge-centered outcomes with the corresponding diminution of affective, or self-concept, categories, and this raised questions about how outcomes can be most effectively organized by sequence or pattern. Similarities in the categories of the two manuals raised questions about the distinction between behavioral outcomes and changes in a person. This led to considering various relations between P and B, e.g., different Bs for different Ps.

**Comparisons with Explicit Objectives**

Many teachers found this exercise similar to their experience in defining objectives before planning a lesson or unit. One participant's list was strikingly similar to the Bloom taxonomy, and he explained, "My Board takes the Bloom taxonomy very seriously." Sometimes our implicit concepts are indistinguishable from the formal reasons. I concluded the discussion by using their concepts to exemplify the process-content distinction in outcomes (Hunt & Sullivan, 1974, Chapter 3), noting its similarity to the developmental-contemporaneous distinction in persons.

## Step 6:
## Identifying Your Concept of Approaches (E)

[See miniature exercise instructions in Chapter 4.] Consider two persons circled in 1−4−8, and answer the question "How are these two alike in terms of how I would work with them?" Record your approach and continue with the other nine pairs.

**Feedback and Discussion**

Feedback sheets showed that participants' E concepts varied considerably in their formality, with counselors using more technical descriptions, e.g., "behavior modification," "non-directive," while teachers tend to use more specific, less formal descriptions, e.g., "Let ideas sit with them," "Give them a job to do." This stimulated discussion. The distinction between espoused and in-use was very important here: "I described how I would like to work with them, but I don't think that I actually could." Several suggestions were made to reduce such ideal/actual disparity in practice. Discussion also permitted clarification of the meaning of such approaches, e.g., many teachers used the term "Socratic" to describe their work, but this concept had very different meanings for different participants. On the other hand, the wide range of E descriptions focused participants' attention on new approaches which they might wish to explore further.

Next the manual for coding teaching approach concepts was distributed, and participants coded their 10 constructs according to 13 categories: (1) teacher-student control; (2) teacher-student centered; (3) structure of lesson or procedure; (4) student participation; (5) social interaction; (6) content focus; (7) cognitive focus; (8) developmental focus; (9) value focus; (10) evaluation procedures; (11) teaching aids; (12) creative; and (13) unscorable. This rough manual is also imprecise, and some participants suggested additional categories before tallying category frequencies. The most fundamental issue in discussion of different approaches was "Can we describe our actions in words?" Some argued that since teaching is specific to a context, any attempt at general description is futile. Others (and I was among them) agreed with this context-specificity of practice, yet maintained we must try to put words on it (perhaps in a different form) or else practice remains a complete mystery. Counselors mentioned the use of videotaped demonstrations and audiotaped supervisory sessions in counselor training as examples of the possibility of communicating about practice, and the question of how such verbal and nonverbal actions can be communicated was re-examined with suggestions of comparing E concepts with actual practice.

### Comparison with Formal Teaching Methods

Explicating one's approaches provides an inductive introduction to topics such as methods of teaching. Participants saw their E concepts in relation to pre-service, or more recent, attempts to learn new approaches. They used their own concepts to consider the size of environmental unit (time and space) as well as similarities between educational environments and parental environments (Hunt & Sullivan, 1974, Chapter 4).

## Step 7:
## Identifying Your Implicit Theories (B-P-E Relations)

Feedback sheets from Steps 4, 5, and 6 were combined for each participant into a single summary sheet (similar to your second sheet) containing three columns of ten concepts (or ten groups of P-B-E concepts). Participants received these 22 feedback sheets a week before the final workshop session so that we could work with both our own and others' concepts. First, we looked at our own sheet "vertically" and reviewed the nature of concepts in each column, i.e., what categories were used more frequently. Next we tried a "horizontal" analysis, identical to the instructions for Step 7; as you must have discovered, this is not easy. Participants were first asked to search for the "relation" between the specific concepts in each row (this could be P-B or P-E), and when a relation was observed in one row, to consider other rows for reoccurrences of this relation. Participants were asked to record their theories, though these were not circulated. Here is one participant's summary, which was read to the group:

> I think that the underlying matching model is if the student has difficulty with affect, then this issue must be dealt with, while the student who can deal with affect can focus on developing skills.

After listening to this theory, we each searched the other 210 triads for examples of this kind of "affect-skill" matching. This focused search for a specific relation also facilitated participants' discovering other relations in their own or others' theories. In fact, some participants identified the theories in others' concepts before they discovered the relations in their own. The discussion became increasingly complex and relational, exemplified by the use of such terms as "filling in the gap" or "playing to strength."

## Comparison with Explicit Matching Models

I mentioned earlier that implicit theories may become indistinguishable from formal theories so I had cautioned other participants not to be unduly influenced by the Conceptual Level matching model which I stated formally (Hunt, 1971) simply because I was also the professor. Nevertheless, several participants "discovered" in their concepts a similar relation between student and need for structure (P) and degree of teacher support (E); this opened the discussion to how formal theories and teachers' implicit theories influence one another. I used the feedback sheets to illustrate various P-E models, e.g., compensatory, remedial, preferential, and other ATI models (Hunt & Sullivan, 1974, Chapter 5).

# References

Abbey, D.S., Hunt, D.E., & Weiser, J.C. (1985). Variations on a theme by Kolb: A new perspective for understanding counselling and supervision. *The Counselling Psychologist, 13,* 477–501.
Argyris, C., & Schon, D.A. (1974). *Theory into practice: Increasing professional effectiveness.* San Francisco: Jossey Bass.
Bandler, R., & Grinder, J. (1979). *Frogs into princes.* Moab, Utah: Real People Press.
Bandura, A., & Walters, R.H. (1963). *Social learning and personality development.* New York: Holt, Rinehart, & Winston.
Bannister, D., & Fransella, F. (1971). *Inquiring man: The theory of personal constructs.* Middlesex, England: Penguin.
Bell, R.Q. (1968). A reinterpretation of the direction of effects in studies of socialization. *Psychological Review, 73,* 81–95.
Berman, P., & McLaughlin, M.W. (1978). *Federal programs supporting educational change, Vol. VIII: Implementing and sustaining innovations.* Santa Monica, CA: The Rand Corporation.
Berne, E. (1964). *Games people play.* New York: Grove Press.
Bettelheim, B. (1983). *Freud and man's soul.* New York: Knox.
Bird, T. (1984). Mutual adaptation and mutual accomplishment: Images of change in a field experiment. *Teachers College Record, 86,* 68–83.
Brandt, L.W. (1983). *Psychologist caught: A psychology of psychology.* Toronto: University of Toronto Press.
Bray, S.A. (1986). *Exploring the instructional process in a professional school: A study of instructors' thinking during teaching.* Unpublished doctoral thesis. University of Toronto, Toronto, Ontario.
Chapman, S.L.G. (1971a, April) *Values and educational environment in a permissive society.* Address to Deep River Home and School Association.
Chapman, S.L.G. (1971b). Personal communication.
Charters, W.W., & Jones, J.E. (1973). On the risk of appraising non-events in program evaluation. *Educational Researcher, 2,* November, 5–7.
Clark, C.M., & Peterson, P.L. (1986). Teachers' thought processes. In M.C. Wittrock (Ed.), *Handbook of research in teaching,* (3rd ed.) (pp. 255–296). New York: Macmillan.
Cohen, D. (1977). *Psychologists on psychology.* London: Routledge and Kegan Paul.

Cronbach, L.J. (1975). Beyond the two disciplines of scientific psychology. *American Psychologist, 30,* 116–127.

Cronbach, L.J., & Snow, R.E. (1968). *Individual differences in learning abilities as a function of instructional variables.* (Annual Report #2). Palo Alto, CA: Stanford University, Department of Education.

Cronbach, L.J., & Snow, R.E. (1977). *Aptitudes and instructional methods.* New York: Irvington.

Davidman, L. (1981). Learning style: The myth, the panacea, the wisdom. *Phi Delta Kappan, 62,* 641–648.

Eisner, E. (1984). Can educational research inform educational practice? *Phi Delta Kappan, 65,* 447–452.

Elliott, J. (1976). Developing hypotheses about classrooms from teachers' practical constructs. *Interchange, 7* (2), 2–22.

Festinger, L. (1957). *A theory of cognitive dissonance.* New York: Harper & Row.

Fiedler, M.L. (1975). Bidirectionality of influence in classroom interaction. *Journal of Educational Psychology, 67,* 734–744.

Fox, D. (1983). Personal theories of reading. *Studies in Higher Education, 8,* 151–163.

Gilligan, C. (1982). *In a different voice: Psychological theory and women's development.* Cambridge: Harvard University Press.

Glaser, R. (1972). Individual and learning: The new aptitudes. *Educational Researcher, 1,* 5–12.

Gregorc, A. (1982). Learning style/brain research: Harbinger of an emerging psychology. In NASSP, *Student learning styles and brain behavior* (pp. 3–10). Reston, VA: NASSP.

Harvey, O.J., Hunt, D.E., & Schroder, H.M. (1961). *Conceptual systems and personality organization.* New York: John Wiley & Sons.

Heider, F. (1958). *The psychology of interpersonal relations.* New York: John Wiley & Sons.

Hookey, M.R. (1985). *Educational consultation: Reflections of teachers and resource personnel.* Unpublished doctoral dissertation, University of Toronto, Toronto, Ontario.

Hunt, D.E. (1951). *Studies in the role concept repertory: Conceptual consistency.* Unpublished master's thesis, Ohio State University, Columbus, Ohio.

Hunt, D.E. (1953). *Change in goal object preference as a function of expectation for social reinforcement.* Unpublished doctoral dissertation, Ohio State University, Columbus, Ohio.

Hunt, D.E. (1955). Changes in goal-object preference as a function of expectancy for social reinforcement. *Journal of Abnormal and Social Psychology, 50,* 372–377.

Hunt, D.E. (1966a). A conceptual systems change model and its application to education. In O.J. Harvey (Ed.), *Experience, structure, and adaptability.* New York: Springer.

Hunt, D.E. (1966b). A model for analyzing the training of training agents. *Merrill-Palmer Quarterly, 12,* 138–156.

Hunt, D.E. (1970). Adaptability in interpersonal communication among training agents. *Merrill-Palmer Quarterly, 16,* 325–344.

Hunt, D.E. (1971). *Matching models in education.* Toronto: Ontario Institute for Studies in Education.

# References

Hunt, D.E. (1975). *Characterization of Thornlea*. Toronto: Ontario Institute for Studies in Education, unpublished final report.

Hunt, D.E. (1976a). Teachers are psychologists, too: On the application of psychology to education. *Canadian Psychological Review, 17,* 210–218.

Hunt, D.E. (1976b). Teachers' adaptation: "Reading" and "flexing" to students. *Journal of Teacher Education, 27,* 268–275.

Hunt, D.E. (1977a). The problem of three populations. In S. Miezitis & M. Orme (Eds.), *Current trends and new perspectives in school psychology* (pp. 51–58). Toronto: Ontario Institute for Studies in Education.

Hunt, D.E. (1977b). Theory-to-practice as persons-in-relation. *Ontario Psychologist, 9,* 52–62.

Hunt, D.E. (1978a). Theorists are persons, too: On preaching what you practice. In C. Parker (Ed.), *Encouraging student development in college* (pp. 250–266). Minneapolis: University of Minnesota Press.

Hunt, D.E. (1978b). *Practice makes perfect? No, practice makes theory.* Keynote address to National Association of Research in Science Teaching, Toronto, Ontario.

Hunt, D.E. (1978c). Inservice training as persons-in-relation. *Theory Into Practice, 17,* 239–244.

Hunt, D.E. (1979). The new Three R's in person-environment interaction: Responsiveness, reciprocality, and reflexivity. *Dutch Journal of Educational Research, 4,* 184–190.

Hunt, D.E. (1980a). How to be your own best theorist. *Theory Into Practice, 19* (September), 287–293.

Hunt, D.E. (1980b). From single variable to persons-in-relation. In L. Fyans (Ed.), *Achievement motivation: Recent trends in history and research* (pp. 447–456). New York: Plenum.

Hunt, D.E. (1980c). *Studies in mutual adaptation.* (Progress report #2). Toronto: Ontario Institute for Studies in Education.

Hunt, D.E. (1982a). The practical value of learning style ideas. In NASSP, *Student learning styles and brain behavior* (pp. 87–91). Reston, VA: NASSP.

Hunt, D.E. (1982b). *Studies in mutual adaptation.* (Progress report #4). Toronto: Ontario Institute for Studies in Education.

Hunt, D.E. (1983a). Reflections of a Conceptual Systems Theorist. *Impact, 18,* 11–17.

Hunt, D.E. (1983b). *A teacher-based approach to learning style informed education.* Paper presented at symposium on learning style, AERA, Montreal, Quebec.

Hunt, D.E. (1985). Demystifying learning style. *Orbit, 73* (February), 1–4.

Hunt, D.E., & Gow, J. (1984). How to be your own best theorist II. *Theory Into Practice, 18,* 64–71.

Hunt, D.E., & Hardt, R.H. (1967, April). *The role of Conceptual Level and program structure in Summer Upward Bound programs.* Paper presented at Eastern Psychological Association meeting, Boston, MA.

Hunt, D.E., & Schroder, H.M. (1958). Assimilation, failure-avoidance, and anxiety. *Journal of Consulting Psychology, 22,* 39–44.

Hunt, D.E., & Sullivan, E.V. (1974). *Between psychology and education.* Hinsdale, IL: Dryden Press.

Hunt, J.M. (1961). *Intelligence and experience.* New York: Ronald Press.

Joynson, R.B. (1974). *Psychology and common sense.* London: Routledge & Kegan Paul.

Keefe, J.W. (Ed.). (1979). *Student learning style: Diagnosing and prescribing programs.* Reston, VA: NASSP.

Kelly, G.A. (1955). *The psychology of personal constructs.* New York: Norton.

Kirschenbaum, H. (1979). *On becoming Carl Rogers.* New York: Delacorte.

Kluckhohn, C., & Murray, H. (Eds.) (1949). *Personality in nature, society, and culture.* New York: Knopf.

Kohlberg, L. (1984). *The psychology of moral development: The nature and validity of moral stages.* San Francisco: Harper & Row.

Kohler, W. (1947.) *Gestalt psychology.* New York: Liveright.

Kolb, D.A. (1971). *Individual learning styles and the learning process.* (Report 535-71). Cambridge: Massachusetts Institute of Technology.

Kolb, D.A. (1975). Toward an applied theory of experiential learning. In C. Cooper (Ed.), *Studies of group process* (pp. 33–57). New York: John Wiley & Sons.

Kolb, D.A. (1976). *The learning style inventory.* Boston: McBer & Co.

Kolb, D.A. (1984). *Experiential learning.* Englewood Cliffs, NJ: Prentice-Hall.

Kolb, D.A., Wolfe, D., et al. (1981). *Professional education and career development: A cross-sectional study of adaptive competencies in experiential learning.* (Contract NIE G77–0053). Washington, D.C.: National Institute of Education.

Kusler, G.E. (1982). Getting to know you. In NASSP, *Student learning styles and brain behavior* (pp. 11–14). Reston, VA: NASSP.

Landfield, A.W. (1954). A movement interpretation of threat. *Journal of Abnormal and Social Psychology, 49,* 529–532.

Lawrence, G. (1982). Personality structure and learning style uses of the Myers-Briggs Type indicator. In NASSP, *Student learning styles and brain behavior* (pp. 92–105). Reston, VA: NASSP.

Lewin, K. (1951). *Field theory in social science.* New York: Harper Torchbooks.

Little, J.W. (1984). Seductive images and organizational realities in professional development. *Teachers College Record, 86,* 84–102.

MacMurray, J. (1961). *Persons in relation.* London: Faber & Faber.

McCarthy, B. (1982). Improving staff development through CBAM and 4 Mat. *Educational Leadership, 40,* 20–25.

McLaughlin, M.W. (1976). Implementation as mutual adaptation: Change in classroom organization. *Teachers College Record, 78,* 339–351.

McLaughlin, M.W., & Marsh, D.D. (1978). Staff development and school change. *Teachers College Record, 80,* 69–94.

Miller, A. (1981). Conceptual matching models and interaction research. *Review of Educational Research, 51,* 33–84.

NASSP. (1982). *Student learning styles and brain behavior.* Reston, VA: NASSP.

Progoff, I. (1975). *At a journal workshop.* New York: Dialogue House Library.

Rotter, J.B. (1954). *Social learning and clinical psychology.* New York: Prentice-Hall.

Rotter, J.B. (1966). Generalized expectancies for internal vs external control of reinforcements. *Psychological Monographs, 80,* No. 28.

# References

Russell, R. (1972). *Bird lives.* New York: Dial.
Ryle, G. (1949). *The concept of mind.* London: Hutchinson University Library.
Salomon, G. (1971). *Heuristics for the generalization of Aptitude-Treatment-Interaction hypotheses.* Paper presented at AERA meeting, New York.
Sarason, S.B. (1954). *The clinical interaction.* New York: Harper.
Sarason, S.B. (1972). *The creation of settings and future societies.* San Francisco: Jossey-Bass.
Sarason, S.B. (1978). The nature of problem solving in social action. *American Psychologist, 33,* 370–380.
Sarason, S.B. (1981). *Psychology misdirected.* New York: The Free Press.
Sarason, S.B. (1982). *The culture of the school and the problem of change* (2nd Ed.). Boston: Allyn & Bacon.
Schon, D. (1983). *The reflective practitioner.* New York: Basic Books.
Schroder, H.M., & Hunt, D.E. (1957). Failure-avoidance in situational interpretation and problem solving. *Psychological Monographs, 71* (3, Whole No. 432).
Schroder, H.M., & Hunt, D.E. (1958). Dispositional effects upon conformity at different levels of discrepancy. *Journal of Personality, 26,* 243–258.
Shulman, L.S. (1970). Reconstruction of educational research. *Review of Educational Research, 40,* 371–396.
Silverstein, S. (1974). *Where the sidewalk ends.* New York: Harper & Row.
Snow, R.E. (1970). Research on media and aptitude. *Bulletin of the School of Education, Indiana University, 46,* 63–89.
Snow, R.E. (1977). Individual differences and instructional theory. *Educational Researcher, 6* (11), 11–15.
Stern, G.G. (1961). Environments for learning. In N. Sanford (Ed.), *The American college.* New York: John Wiley & Sons.
Taft, R. (1979). Review of C. Parker (Ed.), Encouraging development in college students. *Educational Researcher,* (June), 23–25.
*Theory Into Practice, 23,* Winter, 1984.
Watson, N. (1982). Appendix 1 to Interim Progress Report #4—*Studies in mutual adaptation.* Toronto: Ontario Institute for Studies in Education.
Wittrock, M.C., & Wiley, D.C. (Eds.). (1970). *The evaluation of instruction: Issues and problems.* New York: Holt, Rinehart & Winston.
Wolfe, R. (1963). The role of conceptual systems in cognitive functioning at varying levels of intelligence. *Journal of Personality, 31,* 108–123.

# Index

Abbey, D.S., 44, 145, 149, 155, 156
Aptitude-Treatment-Interaction (ATI),
    45, 74, 171
Argyris, C., 168
Bandler, R., 45
Bandura, A., 15
Bannister, D., 14
Bell, R.Q., 116
Berman, P., 123, 127, 128
Berne, E., 126
Bettelheim, B., 113
Binet, 16
Bird, T., 114, 134
Brandt, L.W., 113
Bray, S.A., 119
Bureau of Juvenile Research, 14
Chapman, S.L.G., 23
Charters, W.W., 27
Clark, C.M., 54
classroom grouping, homogeneous
    by learning style (1971–76), 28
Cohen, D., 107
"common sense" psychology, 113–115
Conceptual Level (CL), 18, 19, 20, 24,
    26–29, 32, 33, 124, 134, 171
Conceptual Systems Theory, 17–19, 160
consultants/practitioners, 85
    primary practice (working with
        students/clients), 85
    secondary practice (working with
        practitioners), 85
consultation, identifying patterns of, 102
consumer thinking, 54
CREATE, 146, 157–159
    *C*oncern, 157, 158
    *RE*flect, 157, 158
    *A*nalyze, 157, 158
    *T*ry out, 157
    *E*xperience, 157
Cronbach, L.J., 45, 46, 47
cross-sectional research, 26
Davidman, L., 49
deCharms, Richard, 29
direct experience, 160, 161
diversity, 38
Eisner, E., 110, 111
Elliott, J., 86
Erikson, Erik, 20
exemplification principle, 87, 109
experiential learning cycle (Kolb), 149
experiment (1948–49), 11
Fantini, Mario, 19
Festinger, L., 113
Fiedler, M.L., 116
Fields, W.C., 39
first person singular, use of, 112
Fox, D., 80
Fransella, F., 14
Gilligan, C., 161
Glaser, R., 46
good practice (1976–present), 29
Gow, J., 49, 58, 66, 75, 77, 82
Gregorc, A., 48
Grinder, J., 45
Hall-Dennis report, 23
    student-centered approach, 23
Hardt, R.H., 21
Harvey, O.J., 17, 160, 161

Heider, F., 113
homogeneous grouping (1962–64), 18, 19
Hookey, M.R., 102
Hunt, D.E., 2, 5, 6, 10, 13, 15, 17, 19, 21, 22, 23, 24, 30, 31, 36, 39, 40, 41, 44, 49, 58, 66, 67, 75, 77, 82, 86, 93, 106, 109, 115, 120, 124, 125, 131, 135, 145, 146, 147, 149, 153, 155, 156, 157, 160, 161, 163, 165, 166, 169–171
Hunt, J.M., 18
Inside obstacles, overcoming of, 34
Inside-out, 2, 10, 11, 32, 38, 39, 45, 54, 55, 106, 112, 113, 119, 120, 128, 137, 140, 146, 160, 161
internship (1952), 14
interpersonal relations
    Easterner, 155
    Northerner, 155
    Southerner, 155
    Westerner, 155
interpersonal transaction, 145, 147
Jones, J.E., 27
Joynson, R.B., 114
Keefe, K.W., 49, 51
Kelly, G.A., 1, 3–5, 10, 12, 42, 109, 120, 166
Kelly's Rep Test, 13, 31, 55–57, 70, 133, 166, 167, 169
Kirschenbaum, H., 108, 112
Kluckhohn, C., 37
Kohlberg, Lawrence, 30, 161
Kohler, W., 114
Kolb, D.A., 42, 44, 117, 145, 149, 153, 161
Kolb Learning Style Inventory (1976), 42, 44
Kusler, G.E., 75, 76
Landfield, A.W., 14
Lawrence, G., 48, 92
learning style, 38, 40–42
learning style (1970–present)
    marketing of, 47

learning style (1985)
    demystifying, 49
learning style models, myths of, 50
    myth of novelty, 50
    myth of unlimited resources, 50
    myth that science will improve human affairs, 50
learning style, mystique of, 51
    brain mystique, 51
    medical model mystique, 51
    test mystique, 51
Lewin, K., 4, 5, 23, 57
    classic formula, 21
Little, J.W., 143
longitudinal research, 25
MacMurray, J., 31
mainstream psychology, 145
Marsh, D.D., 138
matching model (1971–76), application of, 23
matching models, 66, 70, 71, 98
    action, 71, 72
    basic belief, 71
    process, 71, 72
matching process, 39, 40, 45
McCarthy, B., 48
McLaughlin, M.W., 123, 127, 128, 129, 138
metaphors, 75, 77, 78
    matching
        formal or intuitive, 75
        immediate or developmental, 76
        one-way or two-way, 77
        preferred or required, 76
        teacher style, 76
Miller, A., 18
modes of experience
    activating in counseling, 152
    characterizing persons in terms of, 153
modes of experience, identifying, 150, 151
    action mode, 15
    conceptualizing mode, 151
    feeling mode, 151
    reflecting mode, 151

# Index

Murray, H., 37
mutual adaptation
    establishing new roles in reciprocal relationships, 130
    implementation, 127
    initiating collaborative relationships, 130
    studies in (1979–84), 129
Mutual Adaptation Project, 146
    view of interpersonal relations, 146
NASSP (National Association of Secondary School Principals), 47, 49
Neuro Linguistic Programming (NLP), 45
new clinical psychology, 16
New Three Rs, 115, 117, 119, 123, 129, 136, 137
    reciprocality, 116, 132, 136
    reflexivity, 115, 132
    responsiveness, 116, 132, 134
Ontario Institute for Studies in Education (OISE), 22, 29, 164,
Outside-in, 2, 10, 11, 38, 39, 45, 54, 55, 105, 106, 113, 128, 137, 140, 146, 160
Peterson, P.L., 54
populations, three
    client, 86
    consultant, 86
    practitioner, 86
practice-theory relations, 6, 123, 124
    back-and-forth image, 126
    bottom-up image, 125
    top-down image, 124
practitioner-as-consumer, 137
practitioner-as-expert, 137
Progoff, I., 9
    "stepping stones," 9
Project Upward Bound, 20
psychologist-as-expert, 2, 106–108
psychologist-as-person, 106, 107
    resistance to, 108
psychology, 1
    study of human affairs, 1
psychology-as-experiment, 11
psychology-as-science, 10–13, 17, 107, 120

psychology, mainstream, 145
RAND Study, 123, 127, 128, 138–142
    administrator involvement, 138
    local adaptation, 138
    long-term, 138
    organizational support, 138
    teacher-as-expert, 138
resistance, 2, 3, 9, 102, 106, 123
    overcoming, 120
    from Inside, 33, 82
    from Outside, 33, 83
    in changing image of practice-theory relations, 142
Rogers, Carl, 111, 112
Role Concept Repertory Test (see Kelly's Rep Test)
Rotter, J.B., 12, 15
Russell, R., 12
Ryle, G., 125
Salomon, G., 74
Sarason, S.B., 4, 5, 16, 108, 130, 145
Schon, D.A., 108, 168
Schroder, H.M., 17, 160, 161
Shulman, L.S., 16
Silverstein, S., 92
similarities and differences
    in learning styles, 37
Snow, R.E., 45, 46, 47, 108
Social Learning Theory (1953), 15
staff development, 137
    applied to RAND principles, 139
    Inside-out or Outside-in, 141
    mutual adaptation in, 138
Stern, G.G., 76
stingers, 4–6, 17, 29, 35, 37, 46, 57, 87, 109, 123
    basic assumptions, 4
sub-personalities, 34
Sullivan, E.V., 15, 22, 57, 135, 165, 169–171
Taft, R., 33
teacher-as-expert, 140
teacher directiveness, 204
    democratic system, 204
    laissez-faire system, 204
teacher thinking, 54, 55, 119

Thematic Apperception Test (TAT), 16
theories/concepts, implicit (June Gow, 1984), 56, 58, 67
    about my approaches, 60
    about my matching models, 62
    about my outcomes, 60
    about my students, 59
    about my teaching, 58
    identifying my learning style, 63
    restatement "About My Teaching," 88
theories, implicit (Maureen Lanois), 88
    about my work, 89
    concepts of teachers, goals, and consulting approaches, 89
    my matching model, 90
    my metaphor, 90
    my model of teacher development, 92
    reflections on writing letters, 89
    restatement, 92
theories, implicit (Barbara Rosen-Schreiber), 96
    about my work, 96
    my B-P-E concepts, 97
    my matching model, 97
    my metaphor, 97
theories of practitioners, 55
theories of teaching, personal, 80
    growth theories, 80
    shaping theories, 80
    transfer theories, 80
    traveling theories, 80
theorist-as-expert, 137, 140
theorist-as-person, 110
theorist-as-practitioner, 110, 111, 137
theorists/practitioners, 109
theorists/researchers, 105
theory (1949–61), 12
Thornlea Secondary School, 23
    characterization project (1971–76), 24
    major objective
        to foster student independence and self-direction, 24
training agents, 21

Transactional Analysis (TA), 126, 131, 145
Twinning Project, 23, 27
    twinning program (1972–74), 26
UFO Model, 115, 125
Walters, R.H., 15
Watson, N., 131
Wechsler, 16
Weinstein, Gerry, 19
Weiser, J.C., 34, 44, 145, 149, 155, 156
Wiley, D.C., 46
Wittrock, M.C., 46
Wolfe, D., 153
Wolfe, R., 20
workshop purposes and principles, 163
workshop to identify implicit theories, 164
    describing whole concept, 165
    identifying concepts of approaches, 169
    identifying concepts of objectives, 168
    identifying concepts of students, 166
    identifying implicit theories, 170
    introduction, 165
    selecting parts of whole, 165
    settings and groups, 164
Yale (1953–59), 16
Your Own Best Researcher, How To Be, 117
    reciprocity in research: negotiating participation, 119
    reflexivity in research: interview yourself, 117
    responsiveness in research: listen to participants, 118

# About the Author

David Hunt is currently a Professor of Applied Psychology at the Ontario Institute for Studies in Education. In 1984, he received the Whitworth Award from the Canadian Educational Association for a distinguished contribution to educational research. In 1986, he received an Honorary Doctorate of Philosophy from the University of Helsinki. David Hunt has written several books and numerous articles in psychology and education.